INSIDE

LANGUAGE • LITERACY • CONTENT

NATIONAL GEOGRAPHIC LEARNING | CENGAGE Learning

INSIDE

LANGUAGE • LITERACY • CONTENT

NATIONAL GEOGRAPHIC LEARNING | CENGAGE Learning

Acknowledgments
Grateful acknowledgment is given to the authors, artists, photographers, museums, publishers, and agents for permission to reprint copyrighted material. Every effort has been made to secure the appropriate permission. If any omissions have been made or if corrections are required, please contact the Publisher.

Photographic Credits
Cover, Back cover ©Andrew Masur/Flickr/Getty Images. **1** ©Greg Marshall. 3 ©Jeff Hunter/Photographer's Choice/Getty Images. **4** ©Dex Image/Alamy. **5** ©Brandon Cole Marine Photography/Alamy. **6** (l) ©John Anderson/Alamy. **6** (r) ©Darlyne A. Murawsky/National Geographic/Getty Images. **9** (l) ©Les Gibbon/Alamy. **9** (r) ©Douglas McFadd/Stringer/Getty Images. **11** (tl) ©PYMCA/Alamy. **11** (tr) ©Michael Newman/PhotoEdit. **11** (bl) ©Lazyfruit Pictures/Alamy. **11** (br) ©Arco Images/Alamy. **14** ©David Young-Wolff/PhotoEdit. **33** ©J.R. Bale/Alamy. **97** ©Petra Wegner/Alamy. **100** ©Joe & Mary Ann McDonald/Visuals Unlimited/Alamy. **101** ©Gary Bell/zefa/Corbis. **104** ©Mark Moffett/Minden Pictures/Getty Images. **116** ©Blinckwinkel/Alamy. **128** ©Bettman/Corbis. **181** ©Bettman/Corbis. **215** ©Kevin Taylor/Alamy.

WCN: 01-100-473

National Geographic Learning | Cengage Learning
1 Lower Ragsdale Drive
Building 1, Suite 200
Monterey, CA 93940

Cengage Learning is a leading provider of customized learning solutions with office locations around the globe, including Singapore, the United Kingdom, Australia, Mexico, Brazil, and Japan. Locate your local office at **www.cengage.com/global**.

Visit National Geographic Learning online at **ngl.cengage.com**
Visit our corporate website at **www.cengage.com**

ISBN: 978-12854-39037 (Writer's Workout)
ISBN: 978-12854-39068 (Writer's Workout Teacher's Annotated Edition)

ISBN: 978-12857-67994 (Writer's Workout Practice Masters)

Printed in the United States of America
Print Number: 09 Print Year: 2024

Contents

Project 13 Write to Tell What Happened

Project 14 Write About Someone's Life

Project 15 Write as an Advocate

Project 16 Write as a Citizen

Editing and Proofreading Marks

Mark	Meaning	Example
^	Insert something.	This lake is beautful. (i inserted)
^,	Add a comma.	I love to fish but I can't do it often.
^;	Add a semicolon.	I've never seen the Pacific Ocean I've heard it is amazing.
⊙	Add a period.	I love going to the beach⊙
(:)	Add a colon.	The tide comes in at 7:30.
˅" ˅"	Add quotation marks.	She yelled, What a view!
˅'	Add an apostrophe.	Anns pool is never clean.
≡	Capitalize.	It barely rains in the mojave desert.
/	Make lowercase.	I usually sit under Trees for shade.
℘	Delete, take something out.	My friend lives on an islands.
¶	Make new paragraph.	"I just saw a salmon!" I shouted. ¶ "Where?" he asked.
◯	Spell out.	My mom has been to the (U.S.)
^—	Replace with this.	His best friend is a ~~cat~~. (dog)
∿	Change order of letters or words.	My aunt's garden is really ncie, but it takes a time long to water.
#	Insert space.	Whales are mammalsthat live in the ocean.
⁀	Close up, no space here.	I went to the aquarium to day.

Name ______________________________ Date ______________

Analyze a Paragraph

What makes this paragraph a good model? Read the paragraph and answer the questions.

A Land Crittercam

by Alyssa Madison

Greg Marshall has invented the Terrestrial Crittercam, which lets scientists study land animals in their homes. The camera helps people see what the animal sees. This will help scientists learn about animals that often remain hidden from view. So far, Marshall has tested the camera on grizzly bears, lions, hyenas, jaguars, and eagles. Marshall chose these animals because he was able to test them in safe places, like zoos. Testing has shown Marshall that there are some things that must be improved. He must find a way to make the camera weigh less so it does not disturb the creature. Marshall is working to make his camera better. Once he does, there is no limit to what we'll learn about land animals!

Feature Checklist

A good paragraph

- ❑ has a topic sentence that states the main idea
- ❑ contains details that tell more about the main idea.

1. Does this paragraph have a topic sentence?

____

____

____

2. What main idea is stated in the topic sentence?

____

____

____

____

3. How do the paragraph's details tell more about the main idea?

____

____

____

____

4. Should the writer add that Marshall is also a filmmaker for a science news channel? Why or why not?

____

____

____

____

____

State a Topic Sentence

Look at the following writing topics and details. Once you see how the details fit with the topic, write a good topic sentence for each example.

Paragraph 1

Topic: Terrestrial Crittercam

Main Idea: How it's kept clean

Details:

- lions clean camera lens when grooming themselves
- grizzly bears clean camera while swimming
- scientists created a screen windshield wiper

Topic Sentence:

Paragraph 2

Topic: Terrestrial Crittercam

Main Idea: How it works

Details:

- camera uses live broadcasts to send data back
- video and audio information is sent to scientists by a radio
- researchers can decide how long they want to receive live feeds

Topic Sentence:

Name ______________________ Date ______________

Analyze a Problem-and-Solution Paragraph

What makes this problem-and-solution paragraph a good model? Read the paragraph and answer the questions.

Breathing Beneath the Surface

by Fatima Martinez

People's bodies are not equipped to survive underwater for long periods. In order to swim deep under the ocean and study the wildlife there, humans need a way to breathe underwater. That is why Jacques Cousteau and Emile Gagnan invented the aqualung, better known as *scuba*. Scuba divers carry tanks of oxygen with them. A regulator works to keep oxygen safe. It keeps the pressure of the air from getting too heavy. It also gives divers air as they need it. A regulator has two parts, or *stages*. The first stage attaches to the oxygen tank. It brings down the pressure from the oxygen. A hose connects the first stage to the second stage. The second stage brings the pressure down even further. It also provides air. In some regulators, the second stage releases air only when the diver breathes in. In others, it supplies air all the time. Using scuba gear lets divers stop worrying about how they will get the oxygen they need. Instead, they can focus on the fish.

Feature Checklist

A good problem-and-solution paragraph

- ☐ presents a problem
- ☐ explains the problem clearly and in detail
- ☐ presents a solution
- ☐ explains how the solution addresses the problem.

1. What problem is stated in the topic sentence?

____

____

____

____

____

____

2. What solution does the writer give?

____

____

____

____

____

____

3. What details does the writer give to explain the solution?

____

____

____

____

____

____

Analyze a Chronological-Order Paragraph

What makes this chronological-order paragraph a good model? Read the paragraph and answer the questions.

Our Scuba Trip

by Paul Donnelly

I went on a great scuba diving trip with my family this summer. First, we decided we were interested in scuba diving and read articles about it. On the morning of the trip, we drove three hours to get to the ocean. Next, we rented scuba gear and put it on. Then, a scuba instructor told us what to do. After that, it was time to go under the water! While we were down there, we saw a lot of beautiful fish. We even took pictures with an underwater camera. After our dive, we couldn't stop talking about what we'd seen. As soon as we got home, we told our neighbors how much fun our trip was. Maybe next year, we'll go back.

Feature Checklist

A good chronological-order paragraph

- ❑ tells events in the order they happened
- ❑ uses signal words like *first, next, then, after,* and *finally* to show the sequence of events.

1. What does the topic sentence tell you about the paragraph?

____

____

____

____

____

____

2. What is the first event Paul tells about?

____

____

____

____

____

____

3. What signal words and phrases does the writer use to transition between events?

____

____

____

____

____

____

Name ______________________ Date ____________

Analyze a Spatial-Order Paragraph

What makes this spatial-order paragraph a good model? Read the paragraph and answer the questions.

Sea Anemones

by Maryam Jhoshi

Sea anemones are complicated creatures. A sea anemone has a mouth in the center. Around the mouth is an oral disc. Tentacles stick out from the disc. Underneath the mouth and oral disc is a column. Inside the column is a passage like the throats that humans have. The mouth opens into this passage. The passage leads into a cavity called the coelenteron. Digestion takes place there, and gases are exchanged there. There are mesenteries around the coelenteron and one on each side of the anemone. The mesenteries unfold so more tissue is exposed during digestion. That makes it possible for the anemone to take in more nutrients. Anemones look more like plants than living creatures, but they are animals.

Feature Checklist

A good spatial-order paragraph

- ☐ proceeds from a visual starting point to an ending point
- ☐ takes the reader logically from one place to another
- ☐ uses signal words like *above* and *underneath* to show spatial order.

1. What is the starting point of the spatial description?

____

____

____

____

____

____

2. What kind of spatial order does the writer use?

____

____

____

____

____

____

3. What signal words and phrases does the writer use to show where things are?

____

____

____

____

____

____

Analyze a Compare-and-Contrast Paragraph

What makes this compare-and-contrast paragraph a good model? Read the paragraph and answer the questions.

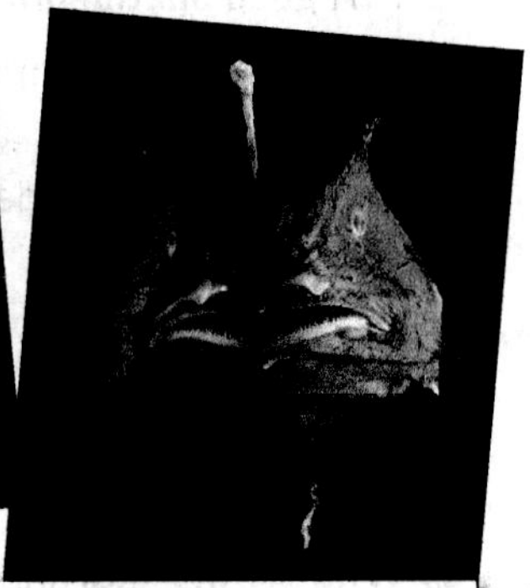

Butterfly Fish and Anglerfish

by Ben Pei

Anglerfish and butterfly fish are similar in some ways and different in others. Many butterfly fish have beautiful patterns. In contrast, anglerfish are known as the ugliest fish on the planet. But the way they look helps both types of fish survive. The patterns on butterfly fish are not just there to look pretty. Many butterfly fish have dark bands across their eyes. On their sides, they have round dots that look like eyes. That way, predators do not know which end to attack. Similarly, anglerfish do not just look the way they do for the sake of looks. Females have a piece of their spines dangling over their mouths. Like the spots on a butterfly fish, this serves a purpose. It lets them hold out bits of flesh so prey will come close enough to be caught. As you can see, these animals that seem so different are the same in many ways.

Feature Checklist

A good compare-and-contrast paragraph

- ☐ names the items being compared
- ☐ describes ways the items are similar
- ☐ describes ways the items are different
- ☐ includes signal words like *both, same, different,* and *however* to show similarities and differences.

1. **What two things does the author compare? Are these things alike, different, or both?**

2. **How are the two things similar? How are they different?**

3. **What signal words does the writer use to make comparisons and contrasts?**

Name ____________________ Date __________

Write a Paragraph

Use pages 7–8 to plan and write a paragraph about your favorite animal.

1. Decide what to write about. List ideas about your topic. Circle the most important idea you want your readers to understand.

2. List details and examples that support your main idea.

3. Think about your main idea and details. Decide how you'll organize your paragraph. Write a topic sentence that reflects your organization.

Topic Sentence for a ____________________ *paragraph*

4. Write your paragraph on the next page. Write your topic sentence and turn your details into supporting sentences. You might want to use a graphic organizer first to plan the order of your details.

Name ______________________ Date ______________

Collect Ideas

Check out the idea files on this page and the next. Add some ideas of your own.

Photos

What our lives would be like without technology

research would take forever

___

___

___

Ways machines can make life easier

___

___

___

___

Quotations

"Genius is one percent inspiration and ninety-nine percent perspiration."

—Thomas Edison

"I believe that if you show people the problems and you show them the solutions, they will be moved to act."

—Bill Gates

___

___

___

Topics That Interest Me

1. How technology is used to solve problems
2. How computers have changed the world
3. Why the Internet is such an important way to communicate

Name ______________________ Date ____________

Collect Ideas, continued

Find Your Truth

Write a truth for each photograph. Tell what you believe is true about the situation.

1.

____

____

____

2.

____

____

____

3.

____

____

____

4.

____

____

____

Choose Your Topic

1. Use the graphic below to help you narrow down your topic. Make it specific enough to cover in a couple of pages.

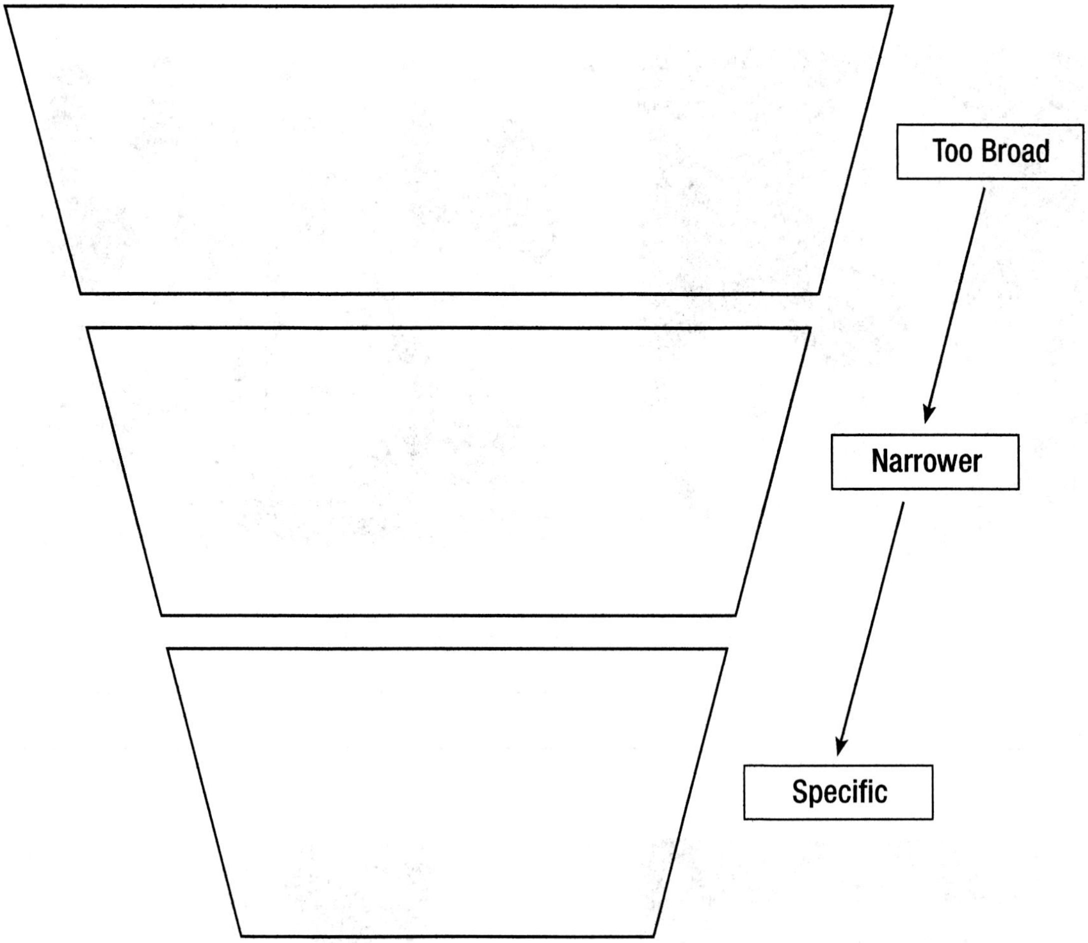

2. What, specifically, are you going to write about? Describe how you plan to approach the topic.

Name ______________________ Date ______________

Choose Your Audience

1. Complete the chart. Write down the tone and give an example of the language that should be used for each audience.

AUDIENCE	TONE	LANGUAGE
your best friend or someone your age	very informal	Hey, Christine. What do you know about solar energy?
an older relative		
your teacher		
someone you do not know		

2. Read the list of people you may write for. Circle the number that shows how often you write for these people.

How often do you write for . . .	Never	Rarely	Sometimes	Often
1 yourself?	1	2	3	4
2 friends?	1	2	3	4
3 family?	1	2	3	4
4 teachers?	1	2	3	4
5 employers?	1	2	3	4
6 strangers?	1	2	3	4
7 someone else: ______________?	1	2	3	4

3. For whom do you most like to write? ______________________

Choose Your Purpose

1. Add examples from your own writing or reading experience for each purpose listed.

If you want your audience to . . .	Your purpose is . . .	Your form might be . . .
· learn something new · understand something better	to inform or explain	informative paragraph
· laugh · feel deep emotion · enjoy reading your work · enjoy reading about a real experience or event	to narrate	
· believe something · take action on an important issue · know what you think	to argue	

2. Study the photo. Choose two different purposes from the chart above. Write a few sentences about the photo for each purpose you've chosen.

Purpose 1: ____________________

Sentences: ____________________

____

____

____

____

Purpose 2: ____________________

Sentences: ____________________

____

____

____

____

____

Name ______________________ Date ______________

Organize Your Ideas

Study the writer's FATP chart and notes. Then organize the information in different ways.

FATP Chart

Form: problem-and-solution paper

Audience: classmates

Topic: the Taj Mahal has been severely damaged over the years

Purpose: to make a claim and support it with reasons and evidence

Notes About the Topic

- Taj Mahal built over 350 years ago on the banks of the Yamuna River in Agra, India
- outer surfaces of the building damaged by recent pollution
- 19th century British colonists chipped away precious stones from inside the building
- in late 18th century, a large silver door leading into the building was stolen

1. Use the space below to organize the notes in logical order.

Topic sentence: Over many centuries, the Taj Mahal has been severely damaged by theft and pollution.

Details:

2. Use the graphic organizer to organize the notes in chronological order.

3. Draw and label a picture to organize the notes in spatial order.

4. What problem and solution will you write about? Complete the FATP chart. Then complete a graphic organizer to shape your thinking. Does the organizer go well with your purpose and your form?

FATP Chart

Form: ______________________

Audience: ______________________

Topic: ______________________

Purpose: ______________________

____

____

Name ____________________ Date ____________

Draft Your Paragraphs

Use your plan from page 16 to write the first draft of your problem-and-solution paper.

Drafting Checklist

- ❑ Show the topic in the title.
- ❑ Introduce the claim in the first sentence.
- ❑ Include logical reasons and relevant evidence to support the claim.
- ❑ Conclude with a sentence that follows from and supports the claim presented.
- ❑ Set down ideas quickly, without worrying about spelling or grammar mistakes.

Name ______________________ Date ______________

Get Ready to Revise

Evaluate the Writing

The writer of the passage below plans to read her work aloud to her classmates. Her purpose is to inform them about a girl who solved a problem by inventing a useful product. Read the paper aloud to yourself. Consider the audience and purpose, as well as other aspects of the writing. Make notes on feedback you would give to the writer of these paragraphs.

Convenience: The Mother of Invention

Convenience is the mother of inventions. Six-year-old Suzanna Goodin loved her cats, but she hated feeding them because washing the dirty spoon was smelly and messy. Suzanna decided to come up with another way to get the food out of the can. She wished her cats ate dry food so that washing the spoon would not be a problem. She thought an edible spoon would be a great idea.

Suzanna worked with her grandmother on a design. The spoon had to taste good and get the food out of the can. Suzanna baked dough into small spoon shapes. After scooping the food out of the can, she could just drop the spoon into the bowl. Suzanna had invented a spoon that made feeding her cats clean and convenient. Her cats liked the garlic flavor the best.

My Feedback to the Writer

Gather Ideas

Use this page to think about your writing, get feedback, and plan what changes you'll make to your paper.

1. Read your paper to yourself. What parts sound good to you? What parts need more work? Why? ______________________________

2. Read your paper aloud to one peer and one adult. Write down any answers you can use to revise your paper. ______________________________

3. Have a peer conference. Use the feedback you get to answer these questions:

What's the best thing about your writing? ______________________________

What do you need to work on to improve your writing? ______________________________

What other changes did your reader suggest? ______________________________

4. Now you're ready to decide how you will revise your paper. Describe the changes you plan to make. ______________________________

Name ______________________ Date ____________

Revision in Action

1. Use the checklist to evaluate this draft of a problem-solution paper. What changes are needed?

____

____

____

____

____

____

Revising Checklist

- ☐ Is your claim clear?
- ☐ Do you need to add reasons or evidence to support your claim?
- ☐ Are there any unimportant or repeated details you could take out?

2. Revise this draft. Use revising marks to show your changes.

Revising

MARK	WHAT IT MEANS
∧	Insert something.
↶	Move to here.
⌐	Replace with this.
ℓ	Take out.
¶	Make a new paragraph.

Convenience: The Mother of Invention

Convenience is the mother of inventions. Six-year-old Suzanna Goodin loved her cats, but she hated feeding them because washing the dirty spoon was smelly and messy. Suzanna decided to come up with another way to get the food out of the can. She wished her cats ate dry food so that washing the spoon would not be a problem. She thought an edible spoon would be a great idea.

Suzanna worked with her grandmother on a design. The spoon had to taste good and get the food out of the can. Suzanna baked dough into small spoon shapes. After scooping the food out of the can, she could just drop the spoon into the bowl. Suzanna had invented a spoon that made feeding her cats clean and convenient. Her cats liked the garlic flavor the best.

3. Now use the checklist to help you revise the draft of your paper on pages 17–18.

Edit and Proofread

Tools: The Dictionary

Edit and proofread the passage below. Use the dictionary excerpt to help with any misspelled words or words you are unsure about.

A Traveling Machine

I wish I could invent something exellant that would let people travel long distances cheaply and easily. My best friend moved across the country recently. Sure, we can talk on the phone, excepting on weeknights. Once in a while, we might even be able to visit. But it is nothing like being able to run excitedly across the street to show each other something or exchanje secrets. I wish I could invent an excedingly fast machine that would let me jump across the country, talk to him, and come back in time for school the next day!

exceeding • excommunicate **330**

ex•ceed•ing \ik-ˈsēd-ing\ *adj* : exceptional in amount, quality, or degree ⟨*exceeding* darkness⟩

ex•ceed•ing•ly \ik-ˈsēd-ing-lē\ *also* **exceeding** *adv* : to an extreme degree : EXTREMELY ⟨an *exceedingly* fine job⟩

ex•cel \ik-ˈsel\ *vb* **ex•celled; ex•cel•ling** : to be superior : surpass in accomplishment or achievement ⟨*excels* in mathematics⟩ ⟨*excelled* her classmates⟩ [Latin *excellere,* from *ex-* + *-cellere* "to rise, project"] ***synonyms*** see EXCEED

ex•cel•lence \ˈek-sə-ləns, -sləns\ *n* **1** : the quality of being excellent **2** : an excellent or valuable quality : VIRTUE **3** : EXCELLENCY 2

ex•cel•len•cy \-sə-lən-sē, -slən-\ *n, pl* **-cies** **1** : outstanding or valuable quality — usually used in plural **2** — used as a form of address for a high dignitary of state (as a foreign ambassador) or church (as a Roman Catholic bishop) ⟨Your *Excellency*⟩

ex•cel•lent \ˈek-sə-lənt, -slənt\ *adj* : very good of its kind : FIRST-CLASS — **ex•cel•lent•ly** *adv*

ex•cel•si•or \ik-ˈsel-sē-ər\ *n* : fine curled wood shavings used especially for packing fragile items [trade name, from Latin, "higher," from *excelsus* "high," from *excellere* "to excel"]

[1]**except** *also* **ex•cept•ing** *prep* : with the exclusion or exception of ⟨everybody *except* you⟩ ⟨open daily *except* Sundays⟩

[2]**ex•cept** \ik-ˈsept\ *vt* : to take or leave out from a number or a whole : EXCLUDE, OMIT [Medieval French *excepter,* from Latin

[1]**except** *also* **ex•cept•ing** *prep* : with the exclusion or exception of ⟨everybody *except* you⟩ ⟨open daily *except* Sundays⟩

[2]**ex•cept** \ik-ˈsept\ *vt* : to take or leave out from a number or a whole : EXCLUDE, OMIT [Medieval French *excepter,* from Latin *exceptare,* from *excipere* "to take out, except," from *ex-* + *capere* "to take"]

[3]**except** *also* **excepting** *conj* **1** : UNLESS ⟨*except* you repent⟩ **2** : with this exception, namely ⟨was inaccessible *except* by boat⟩ **3** : [3]ONLY 2 ⟨I would go *except* it's too far⟩

except for *prep* : with the exception of : but for ⟨all A's *except for* a B in Latin⟩

exchange *vt* **1 a** : to give in exchange : TRADE, SWAP **b** : to replace by other merchandise ⟨*exchange* this shirt for one in a larger size⟩ **2** : to part with for a substitute ⟨*exchange* future security for immediate pleasure⟩ — **ex•change•able** \-ə-bəl\ *adj* — **ex•chang•er** *n*

exchange rate *n* : the ratio at which the principal units of two currencies may be traded

exchange student *n* : a student from one country received into a school in another country in exchange for one sent to a school in the home country of the first student

ex•che•quer \ˈeks-ˌchek-ər, iks-ˈ\ *n* **1** : the department of the British government concerned with the receipt and care of the national revenue **2** : TREASURY; *esp* : a national or royal trea-

Edit and Proofread, continued

Tools: Personal Checklist

Use this page to create your own personalized checklist of mistakes to watch out for.

1. Look back through your old papers to see which editing and proofreading errors are marked most frequently. Jot down your top five trouble spots.

____

____

____

____

____

2. Talk with your teacher about ways to fix these mistakes, or check out a style handbook for tips.

3. Now, create your personal checklist. List your most common mistakes and how you can fix them.

My Editing Checklist

☑ words I mix up:

Edit and proofread this passage. See how many grammar, spelling, punctuation, and capitalization errors you can find.

The Tricky Part

Proofreading my on work can be tricky. Since Im familiar with my own essay, I have a tendency to read through it to quickly. This can led to missing some major msitakes.

Their are lots of places that mistakes can hide. Finding there location can be easy fi you know where to look. For example I no that I some times missuse the words *there* and *their.* So I read threw my essay one line a at time and make sure I am using those words correctly. I also know I tend to transpose letters when type. I read my essay backword to to look for those mistakes.

I usually to like have a friend proofread my essay. A fresh pear of eyes can help find mistakes I may have missed. I usually asks my friend jessica. When she reads my essay she took her time and looks it over careful. Mosttimes we trade papers, and I will Proofread her essay as well If I knotice that Jessica has made the same mistake multiple times, I make a not. When I'm finished, I tell her" you occasionally forget to add a period at at the end of you sentences. You might want to add that to your personnel checklist.

Name ______________________________ Date ______________

Edit and Proofread, continued

Editing and Proofreading Marks

MARK	MEANING	EXAMPLE
^	Insert something.	My jewelry was locked safely ^in the suitcase.
^,	Add a comma.	"I locked my keys in the house^," I explained.
^;	Add a semicolon.	Locks are a great invention^; they help keep our homes secure.
⊙	Add a period.	I am glad Mr⊙ Yale came up with his invention.
(:)	Add a colon.	We use locks in many places(:) houses, cars, suitcases.
˅" ˅"	Add quotation marks.	˅"Can you help me?˅" I asked.
˅'	Add an apostrophe.	My cousin˅'s apartment is in San Francisco.
≡	Capitalize.	linus yale invented the lock. (l and y marked ≡)
/	Make lowercase.	His invention lets us keep our ~~H~~omes safe.
℘	Delete; take something out.	There were ~~also~~ some in my backpack, too.
¶	Make new paragraph.	"You'll understand when you're older," I said.¶"I bet I still won't bring that much stuff," she said.
⬭	Check spelling.	My cousin is only (eigth).
^‾‾	Replace with this.	The suitcase was on ^~~sail~~ sale in July.
∿	Change order of letters or words.	She and my aunt joked that it wouldn't fit in thier house.
#	Insert space.	I brought a#lot of clothes with me.
⁀	Close up; no space here.	I also had to bring some home⁀work.

Editing and Proofreading in Action

Grammar Workout: Check for Complete Sentences

Check the following sentences to see if they are complete. If the sentence is *not* complete, rewrite it so it has a subject and a predicate.

1. The book the librarian.

____

2. Is my favorite inventor.

____

3. He invented a lot of things.

____

4. Invented the phonograph.

____

5. The girl sitting next to me in the library.

____

Spelling Workout: Check Plurals

Fill in the blank with the correct plural form of the word in parentheses.

1. Jeffrey searched the ____________ of reference books for inventors. **(index)**

2. Out of all the library ____________, this one had the most books on inventors. **(branch)**

3. While he was searching for inventors, he found a picture of Benjamin Franklin wearing ____________. **(glass)**

4. He learned that people living hundreds of years ago didn't have ____________. **(telephone)**

5. Thomas Edison improved the telephone so people could talk across long ____________. **(distance)**

Name ______________________________ Date ______________

Mechanics Workout: Check Sentence Punctuation

Use proofreading marks to correct punctuation in the following sentences.

1. Before telephones were invented, people had to wait for letters to arrive?

2. Do you think people could get an answer right away !

3. I can't believe people had to wait days?

4. Today we can pick up the phone and call someone!

5. I'm glad I didn't live back then?

Check Grammar, Spelling, and Mechanics

Proofread the passage. Check for complete sentences, the spelling of plural nouns, and sentence punctuation. Correct the mistakes.

Editing and Proofreading Marks	
^	Insert something.
^ with comma	Add a comma.
^ with semicolon	Add a semicolon.
⊙	Add a period.
(:)	Add a colon.
˅" ˅"	Add quotation marks.
˅'	Add an apostrophe.
≡	Capitalize.
/	Make lowercase.
℘	Delete.
¶	Make new paragraph.
◯	Check spelling.
^—	Replace with this.
∿	Change order.
#	Insert space.
⁐	Close up.

My little brother loves to invent things. He is only nine yeares old, so his inventions don't always work? The time he tried to invent an alarm clock that wakes you up by tapping you on the shoulder. Built a little robot with an automatic arm. But when the alarm went off, the robot's arm swung out and knocked everything off the table!

He also invented a pen that beeps when it is running out of ink. Problem was, it beeped every time the cap was removed. He has good idese. Maybe one day, he'll invent something that works.

Edit and Proofread Your Problem-and-Solution Paper

Now edit and proofread your work.

Remember to Check

- ☐ complete sentences
- ☐ plurals
- ☐ sentence punctuation
- ☐ ____________________
- ☐ ____________________

1. Use a checklist as you edit and proofread. Add things you are working on to the checklist.

2. Look to see which errors are marked most often. Jot down your top three trouble spots.

   ____

   ____

   ____

3. Ask your teacher about ways to fix these mistakes, or check out the Grammar Handbook for information.

Focus on Spelling

Improve your spelling by following these steps.

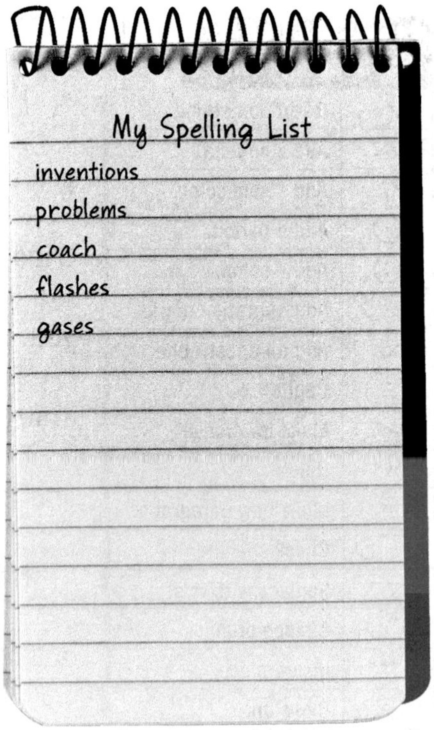

1. Create a personal spelling list. Record words that you misspelled. Look up the correct spelling in the dictionary and add these words to **My Spelling List**.

2. Pick twelve words. Make a colorful display of the words. Write each word three times in a different color on a sheet of chart paper.

3. Work with a partner to play **Spelling Tic-Tac-Toe**. Draw a tic-tac-toe board. Take turns asking each other to spell words. When a player spells a word correctly, that player gets to mark an X or an O on the game board.

4. Write the letters for each word on separate squares of paper. Attach the letters for each word to each other with a paper clip. Unscramble the letters to spell each word.

5. Invent your own memory strategy for difficult words. Think of a good way to remember *why* letters appear or do not appear in a word.

Word	**Explanation**
dessert	"It has two s's for sweet stuff!"

Name ____________________ Date __________

Publish, Share, and Reflect

Publish and Share Your Problem-and-Solution Paper

Check the final formats you used to publish and share your problem-and-solution paper. Then answer the following questions.

Publishing

What was the final format of your project?	**How did you share your project?**
☐ Wrote it neatly by hand	☐ Shared it with a large group
☐ Typed it on a computer	☐ Shared it with a small group

1. Whether you published it by hand or on the computer, what did you do to dress up your final project?

____

____

____

____

____

2. How did you share your work? What did you learn through sharing your work?

____

____

____

____

____

____

____

____

____

____

____

____

____

____

Reflect on Your Problem-and-Solution Paper

Read your problem-and-solution paper. Then answer questions 1–6.

1. What do you like best about your work? ______________________

____

____

2. What did you do well? ______________________

____

____

3. What could you improve about your work? ______________________

____

____

____

4. How did you choose to share your problem-and-solution paper? ______________________

____

____

5. What did you do to make your paper especially right for your audience? ______________________

____

____

6. Will you add your problem-and-solution paper to your Writing Portfolio? Explain your decision.

☐ Yes, I will add this to my Writing Portfolio.

____

____

☐ No, I will not add this to my Writing Portfolio.

____

____

Name ______________________ Date ____________

Analyze a Personal Narrative

What makes this personal narrative a good model? Read the narrative and answer the questions.

My Hidden Talent

by Kia Nakamura

As I stood on the empty stage, I felt my heart pounding through my chest. My hands were shaking and my palms were drenched with sweat. Suddenly my background music started to play throughout the auditorium. At that point I knew I could not turn back. "How did I get myself into this?" I thought. "It was Jaleesa's fault!"

It all started last week. The hallways were buzzing with news of the upcoming talent show tryouts. The drama teacher had plastered neon yellow flyers all over the school, and there was a signup sheet on the bulletin board outside the main office. My friend Jaleesa ran up to me and squealed, "Have you seen the flyers? Kia, you should sing in the talent show."

Those words caused my stomach to do a backflip. I had never sung in public before, much less in front of the whole school. I only sang in the shower, or quietly to myself when listening to my favorite song.

I laughed, "Jaleesa, you must be joking. I could never do that!" I shrugged off her suggestion and went to class, but I couldn't get the idea out of my head. What if I did it? What's the worst that could happen? The day before the tryouts, I ran up to the sheet and signed my name in thick black ink at the bottom. I couldn't believe I was really going to do it.

Feature Checklist

A good personal narrative

- ❑ has a beginning, a middle, and an end
- ❑ includes real events, people, and places
- ❑ uses specific details that let the reader "see and feel" what's happening
- ❑ expresses the writer's feelings.

1. **How does the beginning get the reader's attention? What does it tell?**

____

____

____

____

____

2. **How can you tell that the places, events, and people are real?**

____

____

____

____

____

3. **What details let the reader "see and feel" what's happening?**

____

____

____

____

____

____

____

____

____

____

After a long night of practicing, the big day came. The tryouts were scheduled for after school. It was impossible for me to focus on anything else all day. When the last bell rang, it felt like my death sentence. Jaleesa walked with me to the auditorium, bouncing happily the whole way. "You're going to be great," she said. "Don't worry so much." That was easy for her to say.

I found a seat in the auditorium. There were many others trying out. There was a boy who did magic and a girl who twirled two shimmering batons. A girl from my Spanish class did a comedy routine. She had the whole audience hunched over from laughing so hard! For a moment, I almost forgot why I was there. Then my name was called.

So there I was, standing in the middle of the stage and quietly blaming Jaleesa for suggesting I try out, when something strange happened. As I started to sing, all my nerves went away. Suddenly, I felt like I was just singing in the shower. My hands stopped shaking, and my entire body relaxed. My performance turned out to be a hit! I made the talent show, and the music teacher even asked me to join the choir.

Now I'm glad that Jaleesa encouraged me to try out for the talent show. She saw a gift in me that I could not see in myself. If it were not for her, I would've kept my hidden talent buried under a pile of nerves.

4. What other details let the reader "see and feel" what's happening?

____

____

____

____

____

____

____

____

5. What helps you understand how the writer is feeling?

____

____

____

____

____

____

____

____

6. What is good about the ending?

____

____

____

____

____

____

____

____

Name ______________________ Date ____________

Plan a Personal Narrative

Think of a time you faced a big challenge. What was the experience like? Why do you remember it? Then use pages 33–34 to plan your own personal narrative.

1. Gather details about your experience. Collect sensory details in a five-senses diagram.

I saw . . .	
I heard . . .	
I smelled . . .	
I tasted . . .	
I touched or felt . . .	

2. Now use the sequence chain to organize your ideas.

Beginning

↓

Event 1

↓

Event 2

↓

Event 3

↓

Ending

Name ________________ Date ________________

Draft a Personal Narrative

Use your plan from pages 33–34 to write the first draft of your personal narrative.

Drafting Checklist

- ☐ Catch the readers' interest with your introduction.
- ☐ Include details that let the reader "see and feel" what's happening.
- ☐ Tell about real events in the order they happened.
- ☐ Connect ideas with transitions.
- ☐ Express your thoughts and feelings.
- ☐ End by explaining what you learned, or why the event is memorable.

Name ______________________________ Date ______________

Revise a Personal Narrative

1. Use the checklist to evaluate this draft of a personal narrative. What changes are needed?

____

____

____

____

____

Revising Checklist

- ☐ Are there enough sensory details to help readers picture the event?
- ☐ Does the narrative show how the writer feels?
- ☐ Will adding dialogue make the narrative more lively?
- ☐ Are there any unnecessary details?

2. Revise this draft. Use revising marks to show your changes.

Revising

MARK	WHAT IT MEANS
∧	Insert something.
(move mark)	Move to here.
(replace mark)	Replace with this.
(take out mark)	Take out.
¶	Make a new paragraph.

Climbing to Victory

I looked up at the climbing wall. Even the biggest kids couldn't make it up to the victory bell at the top. And I was the smallest kid.

When my turn came, I started climbing. At first I was a little shaky. I was really struggling to hold on to the pegs and keep my feet from slipping. But after a while I started to get the hang of it, and soon I could climb faster. Then everyone cheered as I reached the top and rang the victory bell. Afterward, I climbed down.

That day, I learned that you don't have to be the biggest to be the best.

3. Now use the checklist to help you revise the draft of your personal narrative on pages 35–36.

Edit and Proofread

Grammar Workout: Check Pronouns

Replace some nouns in each group of sentences with pronouns. Improve the flow of the sentences.

1. My parents told me I might like other activities better than track. My parents said I should try different hobbies. I think I will take up painting. Painting is something I've always wanted to try.

2. Mr. Holtz is my art teacher at school. Mr. Holtz is impressed with my work. Mr. Holtz says I'm naturally artistic.

3. Dad and I are planning to take an oil painting class together. Dad and I start class on Saturday. Mom said that she would get all our supplies. Mom will buy the canvas, paints, and brushes.

4. My family needs some decorations on our walls. Pretty soon, my family will have enough paintings to cover all the walls. Our paintings might be good enough to give to my school, too. Our paintings can be hung in the hallways.

Spelling Workout: Check Plural Nouns

Fill in the blank with the plural form of the word.

1. bay __________	**5.** play __________	**9.** key __________
2. duty __________	**6.** enemy __________	**10.** baby __________
3. toy __________	**7.** chimney __________	**11.** essay __________
4. battery __________	**8.** ability __________	**12.** activity __________

Name ______________________ Date ____________

Edit and Proofread, continued

Mechanics Workout: Check Capitalization of Proper Nouns

Use the editing marks below to correct the capitalization error(s) in each sentence.

1. Assistant coach bezley is just as intense as Coach Johnson.

2. He acts as if we should be the best runners in north america!

3. I want to tell him that we are not running against england, italy, and france.

4. It's just a mesa county high school track meet!

5. I'm relieved he's not going to be at practice next tuesday.

Check Grammar, Spelling, and Mechanics

Proofread the passage. Check the spelling of plural nouns, capitalization of proper nouns, and the use of pronouns. Correct the mistakes.

Editing and Proofreading Marks

Mark	Meaning
^	Insert something.
^ with comma	Add a comma.
^ with semicolon	Add a semicolon.
⊙	Add a period.
(:)	Add a colon.
quotation marks mark	Add quotation marks.
apostrophe mark	Add an apostrophe.
≡	Capitalize.
/	Make lowercase.
delete mark	Delete.
¶	Make new paragraph.
oval	Check spelling.
replace mark	Replace with this.
change order mark	Change order.
#	Insert space.
close up mark	Close up.

My father got his keys, and they was ready to go to painting class. The bartley art school has many activity for aspiring artists. My dad and I had our art supply in my dad's and my bags and were ready to begin. I was excited about the class. I had been looking forward to it since april. I was eager to show my dad my artistic ability.

The instructors loved my artwork. The instructors invited me to enter my work in a contest. It would be held on the last saturday in june. I only had ten daie to prepare! My dad gave me a smile. My dad said "I'm sure your work will be the best out of all the entry."

Edit and Proofread Your Personal Narrative

Now edit and proofread your work.

1. Use a checklist as you edit and proofread. Add things you are working on to the checklist.

2. Look to see which errors are marked most often. Jot down your top three trouble spots.

____

____

____

Remember to Check

- ☐ pronouns
- ☐ spelling of plural nouns
- ☐ capitalization of proper nouns
- ☐ ____________________
- ☐ ____________________

3. Ask your teacher about ways to fix these mistakes, or check out the Grammar Handbook for information.

Focus on Spelling

Improve your spelling by following these steps.

1. Create a personal spelling list. Record words that you misspelled. Look up correct spelling in the dictionary and add these words to **My Spelling List**.

2. Pick twelve words. Write six sentences, using two of the words in each sentence. Wacky sentences are just fine! Double-check the spelling of the words. Then write six different sentences, using different pairs of spelling words.

3. Organize your words into different lists. List your words in alphabetical order. Next list them by the number of letters, from shortest word to longest. Spell the words aloud as you write them.

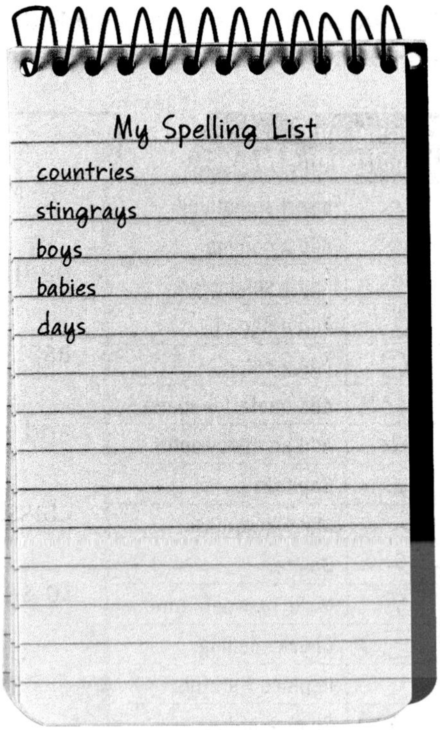

4. Make a personal word wall with your spelling words. List your words on chart paper. Read the words on your word wall. Then spell them letter by letter. Next close your eyes and spell them again, letter by letter. Open your eyes. Did you spell the word correctly?

5. Invent a story to help you remember difficult words. For example:

   Word cemetery

   Story I got scared walking through the cemetery and yelled, "e-e-e!" as I ran away. (The word *cemetery* has three e's.)

Name ______________________________ Date ______________

Analyze a Short Story

What makes this short story a good model? Read the story and answer the questions.

Julia the Great Knot Maker

by Ahmed Russell

The mice in the Abbot house had lived in terror for too long. Ever since Joe Abbot had gotten a new cat, Wiley, their lives had been miserable. Their leader, a sturdy mouse named Fernando, called a meeting.

The mice gathered in a hole behind Joe's refrigerator. The sound of the chatter was deafening to Julia, a small mouse. Julia rarely talked to anyone. She found a small space in the back and watched.

"What are we going to do? My family hasn't eaten in days!" said Mrs. Speck, a plump and friendly mouse.

"She's right!" said Felix, a famous troublemaker. "We're all going to starve! What are we going to do about Wiley?" The mice chattered away. Everyone talked, but no one listened.

"I know what to do," mumbled Julia. Her small voice was lost in the clamor. She gently cleared her throat and jumped up on an empty spool of thread. "I have an idea!" she yelled. Her voice rang out over the crowd.

"Quiet!" Fernando said to the crowd, for this was a special occasion. Julia rarely spoke above a whisper. They turned to her and waited. "What is your idea, Julia?" Fernando asked.

"We could tie Wiley up," she replied. "It would keep him from chasing us." Felix laughed loudly, and the rest of the room softly snickered.

Feature Checklist

A good short story includes

- ❑ interesting characters
- ❑ details about the setting
- ❑ a conflict a character has to deal with
- ❑ a series of events that lead to a satisfying resolution, or ending.

1. How does the beginning set up the conflict? What does it tell?

____
____
____
____
____

2. What details make the characters interesting?

____
____
____
____
____
____

3. What details let the reader "see and feel" the setting?

____
____
____
____
____
____

Julia continued, "Joe's son learned how to tie knots for his camping trip. I watched him every night, and I have been practicing on thread. I think I can do it."

The mice liked her plan, but they decided to try other ways first. Felix made a net and dropped it on Wiley. Unfortunately, the net was weak and the cat broke free. Fernando poured honey all over the kitchen. He hoped it would make the cat stick to the floor, but Wiley just licked it all up.

Finally, it was time to try Julia's plan. Julia tied all the string she could find into one long piece. She asked Fernando to help carry out the plan.

With their string ready, Julia and Fernando hid quietly in the corner of the kitchen. Soon, Wiley entered the room.

Fernando shot out from underneath the refrigerator. Julia had tied the string to his tail, and it flew out behind him like a long flag. Wiley quickly bounded after the mouse and thread.

Julia ran after Wiley, holding the other end of the string in her mouth. Fernando turned left, and the mice ran in opposite circles around the cat. Julia pounced and tied three quick knots to hold the cat tight. Wiley hissed and thrashed his body left and right, but he couldn't untie the knot.

That night, the mice raided the pantry and feasted on treats. Julia sat in a place of honor, and the mice told stories of "Julia the Great Knot Maker" for years to come.

4. What makes Julia an interesting character?

____

____

____

____

____

5. What series of events make the conflict worse?

____

____

____

____

____

6. What is the turning point in the story?

____

____

____

____

____

____

7. How is the conflict resolved?

____

____

____

____

____

____

____

Name ______________________ Date ______________

Evaluate for Organization

Read each short story. Use the rubric on page 44 to score each story for organization of ideas. Explain your scores.

Writing Sample 1

The Bike Challenge

Tyler and Lena had challenged each other to a bike race. Tyler owned an amazing bike. It had big, thick tires with shiny chrome spokes. Also, the wide handlebars made it look like a motorcycle. Sadly, Lena's bike was small and rusty. However, she knew she was a fast rider.

To start the race, they lined up their bikes and waited for someone to yell "go." Immediately, Tyler and Lena were off! They were neck and neck as they soared down the street. Suddenly, Lena's bike chain broke. "You'll never beat me with that rust bucket," Tyler teased as he passed Lena. Tyler won the race with ease.

Score	1	2	3	4

____

____

____

____

____

____

____

____

____

____

Writing Sample 2

Brains over Bike

Lena decided that if she couldn't beat Tyler with her bike, she would beat him with her brain. Lena was upset that she lost a bike race to Tyler. She was clearly a faster rider, but he had a bigger bike. Lena had a great idea.

Lena challenged Tyler to another race. She purposely planned the racecourse to go through a tunneled walkway under the train tracks. The race started. Then Tyler had a big lead. He told Lena she could forfeit the race if she was scared.

Lena wasn't worried about the lead. She knew her plan would work. In the end, a bigger bike isn't always a better bike. Tyler raced towards the tunnel. He tried to make it though, but his bike was too big to fit in the narrow walkway. "Watch out!" Lena yelled as she easily rode through the tunnel and won the race.

Score	1	2	3	4

____

____

____

____

____

____

____

____

____

____

____

____

Writing Rubric

Organization		
	Does the writing have a clear structure, and is it appropriate for the writer's audience, purpose, and type of writing?	How smoothly do the ideas flow together?
4 **Wow!**	**The writing has a structure that is clear and appropriate for the writer's audience, purpose, and type of writing.**	**The ideas progress in a smooth and orderly way.** • The introduction is strong. • The **ideas** flow well from **paragraph** to **paragraph.** • The ideas in each paragraph flow well from one **sentence** to the next. • Effective **transitions** connect ideas. • The conclusion is strong.
3 **Ahh.**	**The writing has a structure that is generally clear and appropriate for the writer's audience, purpose, and type of writing.**	**Most of the ideas progress in a smooth and orderly way.** • The introduction is adequate. • Most of the **ideas** flow well from **paragraph** to **paragraph.** • Most ideas in each paragraph flow from one **sentence** to the next. • Effective **transitions** connect most of the ideas. • The conclusion is adequate.
2 **Hmm.**	**The structure of the writing is not clear or not appropriate for the writer's audience, purpose, and type of writing.**	**Some of the ideas progress in a smooth and orderly way.** • The introduction is weak. • Some of the **ideas** flow well from **paragraph** to **paragraph.** • Some ideas in each paragraph flow from one **sentence** to the next. • **Transitions** connect some ideas. • The conclusion is weak.
1 **Huh?**	**The writing is not clear or organized.**	**Few or none of the ideas progress in a smooth and orderly way.**

Name ______________________________ Date ______________

Raise the Score

1. Use the rubric on page 44 to evaluate and score this short story.

Score	1	2	3	4

Sour Milk

When Bobby O'Shea took over the family farm, everything changed. The O'Sheas used to share fresh milk from their dairy cows with the Murphys. The Murphys used to give corn to the O'Sheas. They were kind neighbors. Their kindness to each other lasted for many generations, but now those kind feelings were gone.

Sally Murphy had trouble keeping Bobby's cows off her farm. Soon the cows started eating up all her crops. At first, Sally didn't make much of a fuss. Bobby was a lazy farmer who didn't like to tend to his cattle. He let his cows roam wherever they pleased.

Sally came up with a brilliant plan. She politely asked Bobby to contain his cows. Bobby suggested it was Sally's problem and she should keep the cows away herself. This angered Sally. She didn't have time to tend to someone else's cows.

The O'Sheas' cows devoured most of Sally's crops. Bobby didn't know that the night before, Sally planted an onion patch along the border of his property.

Apparently, the milk that came from the O'Shea farm that week tasted terribly sour. It was almost as if someone fed the cows onions! Sally heard the town grocer yelling at Bobby.

Bobby O'Shea started tending to his cattle. He kept his cows as far away from the Murphys' crops as soon as possible.

2. Explain what the writer should do to raise the score:

____

____

____

____

3. Now revise the story on page 45 to improve its organization. Write your revised story here.

Name ______________________ Date ____________

Make Your Ideas Flow

Use the sentences to write a paragraph. Add transitions to connect ideas and make the sentences flow.

TRANSITION WORDS		
as a result	immediately	since
because	in fact	suddenly
finally	later	the next day
first	one day	then

Myles was playing basketball outside.

He saw his neighbor, Mrs. Schroeder, walking home from the store.

A gust of wind blew her scarf off her neck and into a tall tree.

It was her favorite scarf. She was very upset.

Myles ran over to help.

He lined himself up in front of the tree as if he were shooting a basket.

He shot the basketball up into the tree and toward the scarf.

The ball landed right on the scarf and knocked it out of the tree.

Mrs. Schroeder was very happy.

She brought Myles a plate of cookies to thank him for his help.

Connect Your Paragraphs

Revise this story. Add transitions from the word bank to make the sentences and paragraphs easy to follow.

TRANSITION WORDS		
at first	but	once
although	however	since
as a result	as soon as	so
because	in the end	then

Bright Baron

Malforth was a dreary city in the center of a mountain valley. Most dwellers wanted to move to the other side of the mountain. The king of Malforth wouldn't allow it. He put a guard at the only tunnel that left the city.

Baron thought he'd never be able to leave Malforth. He had an idea. He did not have much money. He thought he could strike a bargain with the guard.

Baron walked up to the tunnel. Baron said to the guard, "I'll bring you anything you want if you let me pass through." The guard liked riddles. He said, "Bring me something that walks on four legs, three legs, and two legs at the same time. I will let you pass." Baron asked, "If I bring you this thing, may I take it with me through the tunnel?" "Yes," the guard replied.

He heard this. Baron ran home and told his family to pack their things. They hiked up to the tunnel.

They reached the tunnel. Baron presented his family to the guard. "My baby crawls on four legs, my mother with her cane hobbles on three legs, and my wife walks on two legs," he said. The guard was impressed by Baron's cleverness. He let the family pass to the other side of the mountain to begin their new life.

Name ______________________ Date ____________

Plan a Story About a Clever Character

Use pages 49–51 to plan your story.

1. Decide who your characters are and where and when your story takes place.

Setting:

Characters	Description

2. Write down a problem or conflict on which you can base your plot.

3. Then use a plot diagram like the one on page 95W in your book to sketch out your plot. Decide what to include in the beginning, middle, and end.

4. Now use this organizer to flesh out the details of your plot.

Plot Diagram

Beginning

↓

Events Before the Turning Point

↓

Turning Point

↓

Events After the Turning Point

↓

Ending (Resolution)

Name ______________________ Date ____________

Plan a Story About a Clever Character, continued

5. Share your organizer with a friend. Write down any useful feedback.

____

____

____

____

____

6. Find ways to show, not tell, what happens in your story. Gather sensory details in a five-senses diagram.

Five-Senses Diagram

My character saw . . .	
My character heard . . .	
My character smelled . . .	
My character tasted . . .	
My character touched or felt . . .	

Draft a Story About a Clever Character

Use your plan from pages 49–51 to write the first draft of your story.

Drafting Checklist

- ☐ Introduce the characters, setting, and conflict in the beginning.
- ☐ Develop a plot that centers on a problem a clever character has to solve.
- ☐ Keep the story lively by using plenty of sensory details and dialogue.
- ☐ Connect ideas with transitions.
- ☐ Include a satisfying resolution.

Name ______________________ Date ______________

Draft a Story About a Clever Character, continued

Name ______________________________ Date ______________

Revise a Story About a Clever Character

1. Use the checklist to evaluate this draft of a story. What changes are needed?

____

____

____

____

____

Revising Checklist

- ☐ Are the events in a logical order?
- ☐ Does the writing need transitions to improve the flow?
- ☐ Do any sentences or paragraphs need to be rearranged or moved?
- ☐ Does the story have a clear ending or resolution?

2. Revise the draft. Use revising marks to show your changes.

Revising

MARK	WHAT IT MEANS
∧	Insert something.
	Move to here.
	Replace with this.
	Take out.
¶	Make a new paragraph.

The Contest

Hans claimed to be the fastest builder in the county. Another carpenter, Abe, challenged his claim. He proposed a contest. Both men worked feverishly. Hans agreed, sure he could win. Oddly, each time Abe left to get more wood, he returned looking refreshed.

When Abe finished first, Hans was irate, insisting that no one could work that fast. Although Abe's trick was unfair, the townspeople liked seeing Hans humbled. (He was right.)

Little did Hans know, Abe had a twin. The twins traded places each time Abe left to fetch more wood. That way, each could rest.

3. Now use the checklist to help you revise the draft of your story on pages 52–54.

Edit and Proofread

Grammar Workout: Check Subject-Verb Agreement

Complete each sentence. Write the verb that agrees with the subject.

1. The Chief ____________ the contest to the villagers.
   explain/explains
2. They ____________ excited about the contest.
   is/are
3. "The person who collects the most fruits ____________ the winner," proclaims the Chief.
   is/are
4. Each person in the village thinks, "I ____________ the best fruit collector. I will win this contest."
   am/are
5. The villagers ____________ to gather fruit.
   race/races
6. Not everyone wins, but they ____________ a good time anyway.
   has/have

Spelling Workout: Check for Tricky Consonant Sounds

A. For each of the following, write the letters "k," "c," or "ck" in the blank to spell the word correctly.

1. bla____ as night
2. ____ing of the village
3. birthday ca____e
4. for____ and spoon
5. front and ba____
6. winter ____oat to stay warm

B. For each of the following, write a "j," "g," or "dge" in the blank to spell the word correctly.

1. e____ of the paper
2. ____ump into the water
3. bri____ over the river
4. ____am on toast
5. ____enerous in giving
6. ____acket and pants
7. a hu____e elephant
8. ____iant mountain

Name ______________________________ Date ______________

Edit and Proofread, continued

Mechanics Workout: Check Style with Dialogue

Add the correct punctuation to each of these sentences containing dialogue.

1. The Chief in the story was trying to come up with a way to feed his tribe said Mrs. Esposito

2. Miko said It was very clever of him to think of a contest

3. I agree said Marcus but it was Naja and Pando who were the real heroes

4. You're right exclaimed Sam They were the ones who found the fruit

Check Grammar, Spelling, and Mechanics

Proofread the passage. Check the spelling of tricky consonant sounds, the style of dialogue, and subject-verb agreement. Correct the mistakes.

Editing and Proofreading Marks

^	Insert something.
^,	Add a comma.
^;	Add a semicolon.
⊙	Add a period.
(:)	Add a colon.
˅" ˅"	Add quotation marks.
˅'	Add an apostrophe.
≡	Capitalize.
/	Make lowercase.
℘	Delete.
¶	Make new paragraph.
⬭	Check spelling.
⌃—	Replace with this.
∿	Change order.
#	Insert space.
⁀‿	Close up.

The contest are over and the villagers gather around Javi. He have a hudge smile on his face.

"how do you do it?" they ask. "You is a jenius. Can you show us how to catch a lot of breadfruit?

"Sure," says Javi. "Follow me to the tree by the river's ege. I'll show you how to pik the best place to stand."

Javi points up to the breadfruit in the tree. "Just remember that after a dry night, they fall off the tree in the afternoon," he explain. "After a rainy night, they drops in the morning.

Thanks they say. "We could ciss you! From now on, we'll has plenty of fruit on our tables!"

Edit and Proofread Your Story

Now edit and proofread your work.

Remember to Check

- ☐ subject-verb agreement
- ☐ spelling of tricky consonant sounds
- ☐ style with dialogue
- ☐ ______________________
- ☐ ______________________

1. Use a checklist as you edit and proofread. Add things you are working on to the checklist.

2. Look to see which errors are marked most often. Jot down your top three trouble spots.

   ____

   ____

   ____

3. Ask your teacher about ways to fix these mistakes, or check out the Grammar Handbook for information.

Focus on Spelling

Improve your spelling by following these steps.

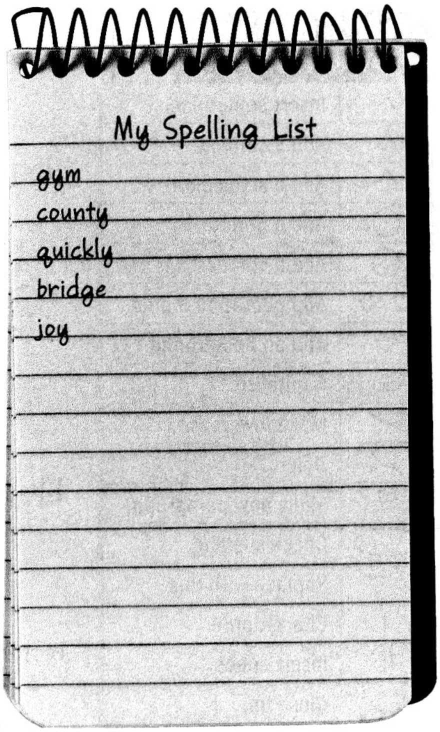

1. Create a personal spelling list. Record words that you misspelled. Look up correct spelling in the dictionary and add these words to **My Spelling List**.

2. Pick twelve words. Write each word four times. First write it in all lowercase letters. Next write it in all capital letters. After that, write the vowels in lowercase and the consonants in uppercase. Last, write the word using fancy letters that you create on your own.

3. Work with a partner to play **I'm Thinking of a Spelling Word**. Take turns giving each other clues. Some clues might be *I'm thinking of a word that rhymes with . . .*, *I'm thinking of a word that begins with . . .*, or *I'm thinking of a word that means . . .* With each clue, the answer should include the word and its spelling.

4. With a partner, play a scrambled-letter game. Take each other's spelling words and write them in scrambled form. See who can unscramble all the words first.

5. Use an audio recorder and record your words and their spelling. Then listen to your recording, checking to see that you spelled each word correctly.

Name ______________________ Date ______________

Publish, Share, and Reflect

Publish and Share Your Story

Check the final formats you used to publish your story. Then answer the following questions.

Publishing

What was the final format of your project?	**How did you share your project?**
☐ Wrote it neatly by hand	☐ Shared it with a large group
☐ Typed it on a computer	☐ Shared it with a small group

1. Whether you published it by hand or on the computer, what did you do to dress up your final project?

____

____

____

____

____

2. How did you share your work? What did you learn through sharing your work?

____

____

____

____

____

____

____

____

____

____

____

____

____

____

Reflect on Your Story

Read your story. Then answer questions 1–6.

1. What do you like best about your work? ____________________

____

____

2. What did you do well? ____________________

____

____

3. What could you improve about your work? ____________________

____

____

4. What did you learn about developing a plot? ____________________

____

____

5. What was the hardest part about creating characters? ____________________

____

____

6. Will you add your story to your Writing Portfolio?
Explain your decision.

- ☐ Yes, I will add this to my Writing Portfolio.

  ____

  ____

- ☐ No, I will not add this to my Writing Portfolio.

  ____

  ____

Name ____________________ Date ____________

Build a Realistic Short Story

1. The events below are out of order. Write each event in the plot diagram in an order that makes sense.

- One day the brothers hit on a great idea: They would make up new games to play.
- Today, Tim works for a company that creates new games!
- Tim and his brother, Chris, grew up in a very rainy area and stayed inside a lot.
- Tim and Chris got to be very good at coming up with ideas and rules for games.
- They tried to come up with creative ways to stay entertained.

Plot Diagram

Beginning Tim and his brother, Chris, grew up in a very rainy area and stayed inside a lot.
↓
Event
↓
Turning Point
↓
Event
↓
Ending (resolution or conclusion)

2. Now that your events are in order, write out the sequence of events as a realistic short story on a separate sheet of paper.

Plan a Realistic Short Story

Use pages 62–63 to plan your realistic short story.

1. Choose a topic for your realistic short story. Think about an event in your own or another person's life that would make a good story. In the space below, quickly jot down ideas you can develop into a story. Circle the topic you choose.

Ideas

-
-
-
-
-

Name ______________________ Date ____________

Plan a Realistic Short Story, continued

2. Use this plot diagram to organize your thoughts.

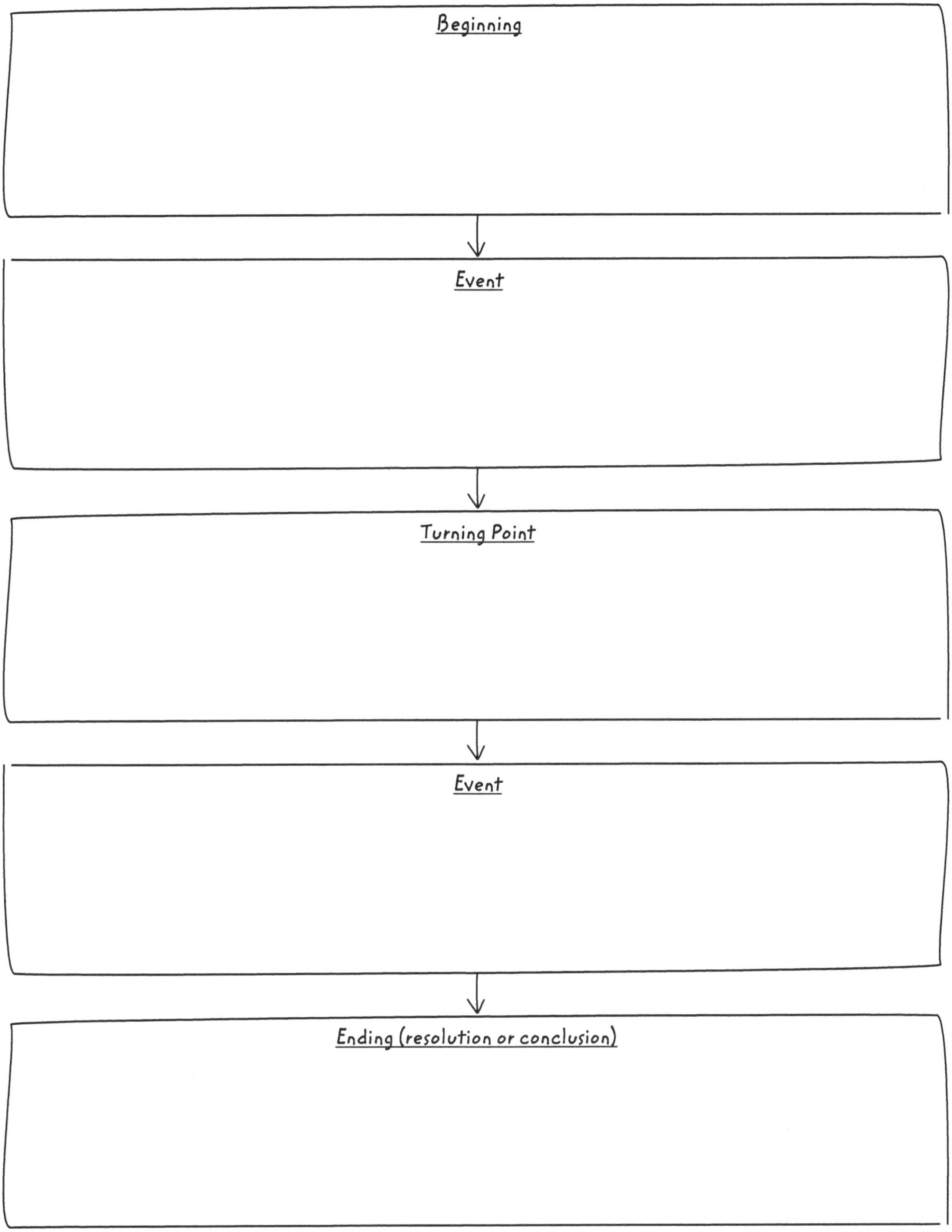

Draft a Realistic Short Story

Use your plan from pages 62–63 to write the first draft of your realistic short story.

Drafting Checklist

- ❑ Create characters and a setting that are realistic.
- ❑ Develop a plot that presents a real-life conflict, or problem.
- ❑ Use a logical sequence of events to show how the problem is solved.
- ❑ Use dialogue and pacing to develop characters and plot.
- ❑ Provide a believable conclusion that follows from the events.

Name ______________________ Date ____________

Revise a Realistic Short Story

1. Use the checklist to evaluate this draft of a realistic short story. What changes are needed?

____

____

____

____

____

Revising Checklist

- ☐ Does the story clearly present events in an order that makes sense?
- ☐ Do you need to add or rearrange ideas to make the story more realistic?
- ☐ Do you need to remove details that are not important to the sequence of events?

2. Revise the draft. Use revising marks to show your changes.

Revising

MARK	WHAT IT MEANS
∧	Insert something.
↶○	Move to here.
⌃‾	Replace with this.
⌒ℓ	Take out.
¶	Make a new paragraph.

Visiting Distant Relatives

Lan recently traveled to China to visit her aunt and uncle. She didn't know much about her family's native country. When Lan arrived at the airport, she was scared. Her cousin Ying came to get her, and Lan recognized her from pictures. Ying was very nice, and Lan learned they had a lot in common. Soon, the girls were able to have good conversations. Ying also taught Lan to speak some Chinese. Lan was no longer nervous about being in a new country. She is glad she visited China because she learned a lot about where she comes from.

3. Now use the checklist to help you revise the draft of your realistic short story on page 64.

Edit and Proofread

Grammar Workout: Check Adjectives

Write an adjective in each blank to make the writing more colorful.

1. Miguel's hands are ____________ compared to mine!

2. His wool sweater felt so ____________.

3. I was ____________ that I might hurt him, but he didn't even seem to notice me touching him.

4. Then, Miguel yawned and curled his fingers into a ____________ fist.

5. He opened his ____________ eyes and looked right at me, and I suddenly felt very ____________ that I was a big sister.

6. I picked up his ____________ body and held him high above my head, jiggling him.

7. He gave me a ____________ smile as he reached out for my face.

Spelling Workout: Check Compound Words

Identify and circle the compound word mistakes in the sentences below. Then write the correct word on the lines provided.

1. One after noon, I was in charge of giving Miguel his bath. ____________________

2. My mom watched closely as I gently placed Miguel into the bath tub. ____________________

3. I was very careful and took my time because I didn't want any-thing to go wrong! ____________________

4. Miguel splashed around like he was in a tiny swimmingpool. ____________________

5. I smiled and watched him closely—I felt like a life guard! ____________________

6. I got him dressed and sat him on the kitchen counter, where he ripped some of the pages in my mother's cook book. ____________________

7. Sometimes he gets me into trouble, but he's the sweetest babybrother there could ever be. ____________________

Name ______________________ Date __________

Edit and Proofread, continued

Mechanics Workout: Check Commas Between Adjectives

Read each sentence. Use the editing marks below to correct any errors in the use of commas.

1. Miguel has a silly, rubber toy that he loves to play with.

2. I place the toy on the plastic, front tray of Miguel's walker.

3. To make the toy move, I tap its white egg-shaped top.

4. The swaying bouncy motion makes Miguel laugh.

5. His delightful joyous laughter makes me giggle!

Check Grammar, Spelling, and Mechanics

Proofread the passage. Check the spelling and the use of commas. Correct the mistakes. Add adjectives to make the writing more colorful.

Editing and Proofreading Marks

∧	Insert something.
∧,	Add a comma.
∧;	Add a semicolon.
⊙	Add a period.
(:)	Add a colon.
∨" ∨"	Add quotation marks.
∨'	Add an apostrophe.
≡	Capitalize.
/	Make lowercase.
℘	Delete.
¶	Make new paragraph.
◯	Check spelling.
∧—	Replace with this.
∽	Change order.
#	Insert space.
⁀‿	Close up.

My parents came to this country from Mexico. They didn't know any body here when they arrived. But after a few days, some cheerful friendly neighbors came by to welcome us.

My mother gave piano lessons. My dad painted pictures. He sold his amazing, landscape paintings to art galleries. At home, they played traditional Mexican music and drew traditional Mexican art. They made Miguel and me feel like we were in Mexico!

When Miguel and I get older, we'll continue to play music and enjoy traditional art work. It's part of our heritage.

Edit and Proofread Your Story

Now edit and proofread your work.

Remember to Check

- ☐ adjectives
- ☐ spelling of compound words
- ☐ commas
- ☐ ______________________
- ☐ ______________________

1. Use a checklist as you edit and proofread. Add things you are working on to the checklist.
2. Look to see which errors are marked most often. Jot down your top three trouble spots.

   ____

   ____

   ____

3. Ask your teacher about ways to fix these mistakes, or check out the Grammar Handbook for information.

Focus on Spelling

Improve your spelling by following these steps.

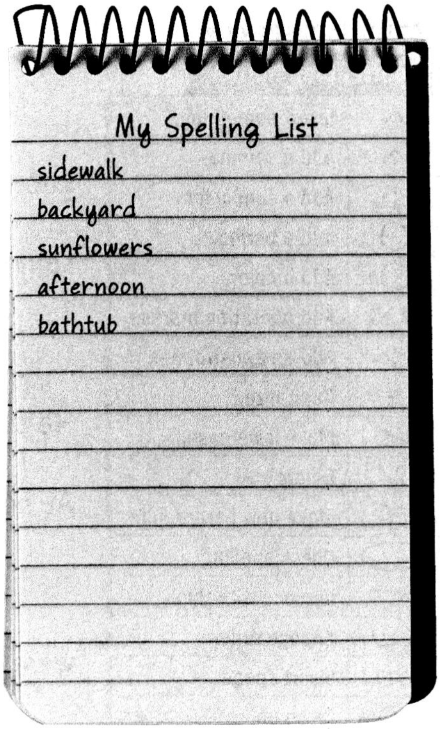

1. Create a personal spelling list. Record words that you misspelled. Look up correct spelling in the dictionary and add these words to **My Spelling List**.
2. Pick twelve words. On a sheet of chart paper, write each word three times in different colors.
3. Work with a partner to play **Spelling Tic-Tac-Toe**. Draw a tic-tac-toe board. Take turns asking each other to spell words. When a player spells a word correctly, that player gets to mark an X or an O on the game board.
4. Write the letters for each word on separate squares of paper. Attach the letters for each word together with a paper clip. Unscramble the letters to spell the word.
5. Invent your own memory strategy for difficult words. Think of a good way to remember *why* letters appear in a word. For example:

Word	Explanation
dessert	"It has two s's for sweet stuff!"

Name ______________________ Date ____________

Analyze a Cause-and-Effect Essay

What makes this cause-and-effect essay a good model? Read the essay and answer the questions.

Russian Immigration

by Anya Borodyansky

Over the past century, there have been several waves of Russian immigration to the U.S. Each time, the emigrants came to America to escape difficult conditions at home and to look for new opportunities.

In the early 20th century, the ruling class of Russia was overthrown as a result of communist revolution. The czar had strict rules about who could leave the country. When he was overthrown, many Russians took the chance to leave. They wanted to escape the violence of the revolution and the social and political problems caused by the fall of the czar.

Under the communists, Russians faced harsh repression. They also faced violence and danger during World War II. In order to escape the repression and violence, many Russians left for America.

After World War II, the Soviet Union and the U.S. were enemies. During this time, the Soviet Union's leaders once again kept people from leaving the country. This caused a low point in Russian immigration.

The fall of the Soviet Union in the 1990s signaled the chance for a new wave of Russians to immigrate to the United States. The country's new leaders lifted the ban on emigration. This allowed a wave of immigrants that continues today.

Feature Checklist

A good cause-and-effect essay

- ☐ presents one or more causes that lead to one or more effects
- ☐ includes an introduction, a body, and a conclusion.

1. What central idea does the writer present?

____

____

____

____

2. What types of causes and effects does the writer present?

____

____

____

____

3. Name an event in the essay that is both an effect and a cause. Explain.

____

____

____

____

____

____

____

4. What are some of the words the writer uses to signal causes and effects?

____

____

____

____

____

Many of the Russian immigrants who came to the U.S. entered through Ellis Island. The island is located at the entrance to New York Harbor. Because so many immigrants came this way between 1892 and 1954, Ellis Island was considered the gateway to the U.S.

A great number of Russian immigrants who arrived in the early 20th century stayed in New York City. Because they came with little money and couldn't speak much English, these immigrants couldn't afford nice places to live or find high-paying jobs.

Many Russian immigrants settled into an economically struggling section of New York City known as Brighton Beach. They brought their music, food, arts, and crafts to the area. This wave of new residents caused Brighton Beach to thrive. In order to serve these new residents, many of the Russians opened stores and earned good livings.

Today, Brighton Beach is known as "Little Russia." The area is a busy neighborhood. You can eat a Russian meal, shop at a Russian store, and hear Russian spoken everywhere you go. The Russian immigrants of the last century have made that corner of New York City a place where they can be free and feel at home.

5. What caused the first Russian immigrants to settle in Brighton Beach?

____

____

____

____

____

____

____

6. What effect did this concentration of immigrants have on the neighborhood?

____

____

____

____

____

____

7. How does the conclusion relate back to the central idea?

____

____

____

____

____

____

Name ______________________ Date ______________

Evaluate for Focus and Unity

Read these samples from a cause-and-effect essay. Use the rubric on page 72 to score each sample for focus and unity. Explain your scores.

Writing Sample 1

Learning English with Computers

Everyone knows that learning to read and write takes a lot of practice. Learning these things in a new language can be very difficult. To ease the process, teachers in many classrooms are using computers to help immigrants learn English.

Computers help English language learners stay interested in their reading. In the past, many teachers gave immigrants English books with simple words and pictures. Older students weren't always happy about reading these books. When books are on a computer, though, students are more interested. Reading on the computer is interactive, and it makes students feel like adults.

Score	1	2	3	4

Writing Sample 2

Computers can also help immigrants write in English. Many people like to use e-mail. It's quick and easy to send an electronic letter to a friend or family member. As a result, e-mail has become one of the most popular ways for people around the world to communicate with each other. Teachers allow immigrants to practice their writing skills by writing e-mails in English. Students enjoy checking their e-mail.

Moving to a new country can be hard when you don't know how to communicate with people there. Friends and neighbors are always willing to help out, though. Because of this, many immigrants are able to learn a new language successfully.

Score	1	2	3	4

Writing Rubric

Focus and Unity	How clearly does the writing present a central idea or claim?	How well does everything go together?
4 Wow!	The writing expresses a clear central idea or claim about the topic.	**Everything in the writing goes together.** • The main idea of each paragraph goes with the central idea or claim of the paper. • The main idea and details within each paragraph are related. • The conclusion is about the central idea or claim.
3 Ahh.	The writing expresses a generally clear central idea or claim about the topic.	**Most parts of the writing go together.** • The main idea or claim of most paragraphs goes with the central idea or claim of the paper. • In most paragraphs, the main idea and details are related. • Most of the conclusion is about the central idea or claim.
2 Hmm.	The writing includes a topic, but the central idea or claim is not clear.	**Some parts of the writing go together.** • The main idea of some paragraphs goes with the central idea or claim of the paper. • In some paragraphs, the main idea and details are related. • Some of the conclusion is about the central idea or claim.
1 Huh?	The writing includes many topics and does not express one central idea or claim.	**The parts of the writing do not go together.** • Few paragraphs have a main idea, or the main idea does not go with the central idea or claim of the paper. • Few paragraphs contain a main idea and related details. • None of the conclusion is about the central idea or claim.

Name ______________________ Date ______________

Raise the Score

1. Use the rubric on page 72 to evaluate and score this cause-and-effect essay.

Score	1	2	3	4

Russian Classes

My mother and my aunt live in the United States, but they were born in Russia. Last year, they decided to start Russian classes in our town. Lots of people like to learn about other countries.

Before the classes started, most of my friends only spoke English. Some of them spoke Spanish or French as well. As a result of going to Russian class, they've learned a few Russian words, too. Sometimes my friends and I say "Preev'yet!" to each other. This means "Hi!" in Russian. Russian words can be hard for many Americans to pronounce.

In Russian class, we also learn about Russian food, landmarks, and holidays. Learning about these things has made my friends interested in visiting Russia. I've visited Russia once with my family, and it was an amazing trip. I got to eat lots of *blini*, which are delicious Russian pancakes.

My mom and aunt love teaching because the classes remind them of their home. They grew up near Moscow. Moscow, a city in western Russia, is the country's capital. It's also Russia's largest city.

There's a lot to learn about Russia. Now my friends want to learn more about other countries around the world.

2. Explain what the writer should do to raise the score:

____

____

____

____

3. Now revise the cause-and-effect essay on page 73 to improve its focus and unity. Write your revised essay here.

Name ______________________ Date ____________

State a Central Idea

Read each central idea for a cause-and-effect essay on the topic of emigration. Does the central idea seem too broad, too narrow, or just right? Check the appropriate box and give reasons for your answers.

1. **Central Idea:** Many people have left their home countries.

   ❑ Too broad ❑ Too narrow ❑ Just right

   ____

   ____

   ____

2. **Central Idea:** Stephanie Bai moved to the United States from Sudan when war broke out near her home.

   ❑ Too broad ❑ Too narrow ❑ Just right

   ____

   ____

   ____

3. **Central Idea:** War causes people to leave their countries.

   ❑ Too broad ❑ Too narrow ❑ Just right

   ____

   ____

   ____

4. **Central Idea:** The war in Sudan caused many people to leave Sudan for new lives in the United States.

   ❑ Too broad ❑ Too narrow ❑ Just right

   ____

   ____

   ____

5. **Central Idea:** Stephanie Bai traveled from Sudan to France and Canada before finally arriving in the United States.

   ❑ Too broad ❑ Too narrow ❑ Just right

   ____

   ____

   ____

Read each set of facts. Write a central-idea statement based on the information provided.

6.

- **In the 19th century, people had to leave Sweden because there was not enough land to farm.**
- **Some people in Sweden were forced to leave because of their religious beliefs.**
- **People from Sweden liked living in Minnesota because it reminded them of home and had many job opportunities.**

Central Idea: ______________________________

____

____

7.

- **Cinco de Mayo is observed in the United States as a day to celebrate the culture and experiences of Mexican Americans.**
- **On St. Patrick's Day, Americans celebrate St. Patrick, an Irish hero, by wearing green.**
- **Many people in the United States celebrate Chinese New Year with parades and fireworks.**

Central Idea: ______________________________

____

____

8.

- **San Francisco's Chinatown is one of North America's biggest ethnic Chinese communities.**
- **San Francisco's Chinatown is the oldest Chinese community in the United States.**
- **San Francisco served as the entry point for many Chinese immigrants between 1850 and 1900.**

Central Idea: ______________________________

____

____

Name ______________________ Date ____________

Stay Focused on the Central Idea

Read these paragraphs for a cause-and-effect essay. Which parts don't go with the central idea? Use revising marks to delete details that don't belong. Explain your thinking next to each deletion.

A Tough Entrance Exam

Between 1892 and 1954, most immigrants entering the United States came through Ellis Island. ~~Ellis Island lies off the coast of New York~~. Because people had to take many tests before they were free to enter the country, the immigration process was often stressful.

When people arrived at Ellis Island, they had to pass a physical examination. Today, most people see the doctor every year. Visiting the doctor keeps us healthy. However, many immigrants were in poor health. Those with health problems were sent away. Because of this, it was very important that each immigrant pass the medical exam.

Many immigrants were hoping to have a better life in the United States. The second stressful test they faced was a series of 29 questions. Immigrants had to give officials several pieces of information. For example, they had to say how much money they brought with them. If their answers to the questions were acceptable, they were allowed into the country. Immigrants who did not pass the tests were sent back to their home countries, places like Ireland and Germany.

The location of Ellis Island does not relate to the central idea of the difficult immigration process.

Plan a Cause-and-Effect Essay

Use pages 78–79 to plan your cause-and-effect essay.

1. First, choose a topic. Think of important events in your community that have clear causes and effects. Brainstorm ideas by asking questions. Record your ideas in the chart below. Then choose one to develop your cause-and-effect essay.

Ideas	Cause-and-effect Questions	Possible Causes and Effects

2. The central idea is the most important thing you have to say in your essay. Write your central idea on the lines below.

____

____

____

____

____

Name ______________________ Date ____________

Plan a Cause-and-Effect Essay, continued

3. Use the cause-and-effect chain below to organize your thoughts and show how each cause is related to an effect.

Event 1

Event 2

Event 3

Event 4

Event 5

Event 6

Draft a Cause-and-Effect Essay

Use your plan from pages 78–79 to write the first draft of your cause-and-effect essay.

Drafting Checklist

- ☐ State your central idea in your introduction.
- ☐ Present and explain causes and effects in the body of your essay.
- ☐ Focus on details that support the central idea.
- ☐ Use signal words to show causes and effects.
- ☐ Sum up the central idea in your conclusion.

Name ______ Date ______

Draft a Cause-and-Effect Essay, continued

Revise a Cause-and-Effect Essay

1. Use the checklist to evaluate this draft of a cause-and-effect essay. What changes are needed?

____

____

____

____

____

Revising Checklist

- ☐ Are causes and effects clearly linked to each other?
- ☐ Is there a clear central idea?
- ☐ Do all details relate to the central idea?
- ☐ Do any details need to be rearranged for a more effective order?

2. Revise this draft. Use revising marks to show your changes.

Revising

MARK	WHAT IT MEANS
^	Insert something.
⟲	Move to here.
^—	Replace with this.
—ℓ	Take out.
¶	Make a new paragraph.

A Celebration of Culture

This year, our school organized a cultural fair. The fair helped our community.

At the fair, people set up booths with information about their cultures. Some people performed traditional dances, and others cooked delicious food from family recipes. I liked the lumpia the best! Everyone learned more about the different cultures in our community.

The whole event was a huge success. We've decided to make it a yearly event. Each year, we'll learn more about our friends' amazing cultures. The fair brought people together in a fun, educational way.

Name ______________________ Date ______________

Revise a Cause-and-Effect Essay, continued

3. Now use this checklist to evaluate this other draft. What changes are needed?

____

____

____

____

____

Revising Checklist

- ☐ Is the essay focused on a central idea?
- ☐ Can you add headings to make clear how each section relates to the central idea?
- ☐ Do you need to delete details that are not important to the central idea?

4. Revise this draft. Use revising marks to show your changes.

Revising

MARK	WHAT IT MEANS
^	Insert something.
↶ (circle)	Move to here.
^‾	Replace with this.
—ᘝ	Take out.
¶	Make a new paragraph.

A Celebration of Culture

This year, our school organized a cultural fair. The fair helped us learn more about our friends and our community.

At the fair, people set up booths with information about their cultures. Some people performed traditional dances, and others cooked delicious food from family recipes. I liked the lumpia the best! As a result, everyone learned more about the different cultures in our community.

The fair brought people together in a fun, educational way. The whole event was a huge success. Because of this success, we've decided to make it a yearly event. Each year, we'll learn more about our friends' amazing cultures.

5. Now use the checklist to help you revise the draft of your cause-and-effect essay on pages 80–81.

Edit and Proofread

Grammar Workout: Check Adverbs

Complete each sentence with an adverb that tells how, when, or where.

1. On Saturdays, our class drives __________ to the recycling center in Roanoke.
(where)

2. It's great that our community has a recycling center __________ .
(where)

3. Mrs. Gomez __________ drives the van to the center.
(when)

4. Just before we leave, we __________ separate our paper and plastic items.
(how)

5. This way, when we get there, we know __________ what bags go in which bins.
(how)

6. Last Saturday, Mrs. Gomez didn't arrive till 9:00, so we started out __________ .
(when)

7. When we got __________, we had to wait behind a long line of cars and trucks.
(where)

8. We were __________ late getting back home, and Mrs. Gomez had to start calling parents on her cell phone.
(how)

Spelling Workout: Check Adverbs Ending in *-ly*

Change these adjectives to adverbs by adding the suffix *-ly*.

1. painful __________

2. active __________

3. fierce __________

4. due __________

5. bizarre __________

6. internal __________

7. youthful __________

8. noble __________

9. true __________

10. casual __________

11. inclusive __________

12. unbelievable __________

13. conversational __________

14. tingle __________

15. horrible __________

16. intentional __________

Name ______________________________ Date ______________

Edit and Proofread, continued

Mechanics Workout: Check Capitalization of Proper Nouns

Use proofreading marks from the chart below to correct the capitalization errors in each sentence.

1. The roanoke regional recycling center is really nice.
2. I read in the newspaper that it just opened last new year's day.
3. The article was titled "A fresh start for garbage."
4. Now we go and help out every other saturday.
5. Last week, the center's director, tasha jones, thanked us for our help.

Check Grammar, Spelling, and Mechanics

Proofread the passage. Check the spelling and the capitalization of proper nouns. Correct the mistakes. Add adverbs to make the writing more precise.

Editing and Proofreading Marks

^	Insert something.
^ (with comma)	Add a comma.
^ (with semicolon)	Add a semicolon.
⊙	Add a period.
(:)	Add a colon.
∨ ∨ (with quotation marks)	Add quotation marks.
∨ (with apostrophe)	Add an apostrophe.
≡	Capitalize.
/	Make lowercase.
(delete mark)	Delete.
¶	Make new paragraph.
◯	Check spelling.
(replace mark)	Replace with this.
∿	Change order.
#	Insert space.
⌒	Close up.

I wanted my school to have a recycling center, so I talked to the principal, mr. currier. He was extremly excited about the idea, but he was worried that no one would use the center. He agreed to install it immediatly if we started a recycling campaign.

I contacted the department of environmental services. They gave me posters to put up around school. I even started a recycling club. I was incredibley nervous that no one would join, but twenty people signed up!

Everyone uses our new recycling center. The school newspaper even wrote an article about it last february. It's really making a difference!

Edit and Proofread Your Essay

Now edit and proofread your work.

Remember to Check

- ☐ adverb usage
- ☐ spelling of adverbs ending in *-ly*
- ☐ capitalization of proper nouns
- ☐ ____________________
- ☐ ____________________

1. Use a checklist as you edit and proofread. Add things you are working on to the checklist.

2. Look to see which errors are marked most often. Jot down your top three trouble spots.

____

____

____

3. Ask your teacher about ways to fix these mistakes, or check out the Grammar Handbook for information.

Focus on Spelling

Improve your spelling by following these steps.

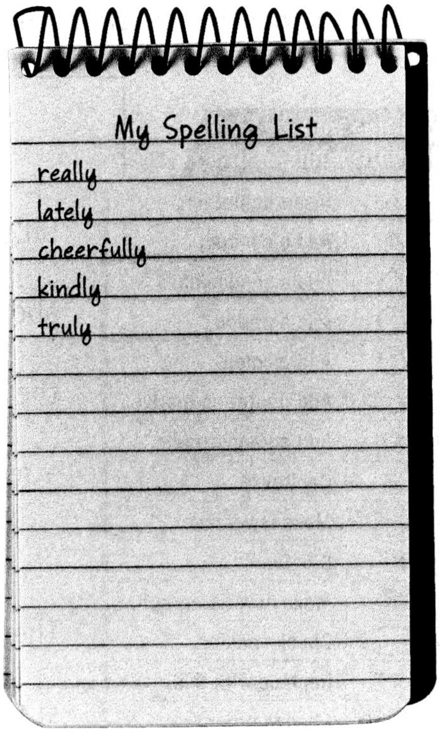

1. Create a personal spelling list. Record words that you misspelled. Look up correct spelling in the dictionary and add these words to **My Spelling List**.

2. Pick twelve words. Make each word look interesting and special by tracing it five times. Write the word in one color. Then trace it four more times in four different colors. Say each letter to yourself as you trace it.

3. Work with a partner to play **Spelling Catch**. Take turns pitching words to each other by saying, "Here's the pitch. The word is . . ." The first "batter" to spell ten words correctly wins.

4. Write each spelling word three times. The first time, just write the word. Then write it and circle all the consonants. Next, write it and circle all the vowels.

5. Play **Memory** to help you remember your words. Write each spelling word on two different index cards. Mix up the cards and place them face down. Turn the cards over two at a time. Your goal is to find the matching cards. Say and spell the words on the cards you turn over. If you make a match, remove those cards from the game. You've won when you've removed all the cards.

Name ______________________ Date ____________

Publish, Share, and Reflect

Publish and Share Your Cause-and-Effect Essay

Check the final formats you used to publish your cause-and-effect essay. Then answer the following questions.

Publishing

What was the final format of your project?	How did you share your project?
☐ Wrote it neatly by hand	☐ Shared it with a large group
☐ Typed it on a computer	☐ Shared it with a small group

1. Whether you published it by hand or on the computer, what did you do to dress up your final project?

____

____

____

____

____

2. How did you share your work? What did you learn through sharing your work?

____

____

____

____

____

____

____

____

____

____

____

____

____

____

Reflect on Your Cause-and-Effect Essay

Read your cause-and-effect essay. Then answer questions 1–6.

1. What do you like best about your work? ______________________

____

____

2. What did you do well? ______________________

____

____

3. What could you improve about your work? ______________________

____

____

4. Did writing about cause and effects help you understand your topic better? ______________________

____

____

5. What did you learn from writing this essay? ______________________

____

____

6. Will you add your cause-and-effect essay to your Writing Portfolio? Explain your decision.

☐ Yes, I will add this to my Writing Portfolio.

____

____

☐ No, I will not add this to my Writing Portfolio.

____

____

Name ______________________ Date ______________

Analyze a Research Report

What makes this research report a good model? Read the research report and answer the questions.

A Wet Nose That Can Save Lives

by Nadia Eilperin

People have always shared a special bond with dogs. Every day, dogs work with humans to complete many tasks. Today, dogs are showing a new, unexpected talent. Scientists discovered that dogs can be trained to detect cancer.

Dogs' Sense of Smell

Dogs have an amazing sense of smell. Scientists even measured it, and found out that it can be up to 100,000 times better than a human's sense of smell (Hauptmann 12). Dogs don't have very good sight (Gomez 45). So they rely on their noses to find food, avoid danger, and get to know the world around them. People have learned to take advantage of their dogs' noses. For example, dogs are used at airports to prevent the trafficking of illegal objects.

A Daring Experiment

Recently, scientists at the Pine Street Foundation of San Anselmo, California have conducted an experiment (Ramsey 66). They wanted to know if dogs could sniff cancer from a person's breath. Apparently, when people have lung or breast cancer, their breath releases certain chemical substances (Cheng 9).

Feature Checklist

A good research report

- ☐ is focused on a specific topic
- ☐ gives information from a variety of sources
- ☐ is well organized, with an introduction, body, and conclusion.

1. What is the central idea of the report?

____

____

____

____

____

____

2. How does the writer use headings in the report?

____

____

____

____

____

____

3. How does the writer provide information about her sources?

____

____

____

____

____

____

____

First, the scientists collected samples of human breath. Some of the people chosen for the experiment had been diagnosed with lung or breast cancer. Then, they selected five household dogs. For three weeks, they trained the dogs to recognize cancer from the samples. They placed the samples on the floor and trained dogs to sniff them. If a dog thought a sample was from a cancer patient, the dog would sit in front of it. The dogs received a treat when they guessed right. The results of the experiment were astonishing. Up to 97% of the time, the dogs were right (Ramsey 68).

Incredible Stories

In the past, there have been many people who were saved from cancer by their pets. In 1989, a British woman went to her doctor because of a mole on her leg. Apparently, her dog was sniffing the mole all the time. The mole turned out to be skin cancer. The mole was removed, and the woman is now safe (Bradshaw 5). Today, stories like this have found scientific proof.

Hopes for the Future

Scientists around the world are very excited about this discovery. "Dogs could offer a reliable diagnosis for cancer," explained Dr. Thompson, who works in cancer research. "Also, we hope to understand how a dog's nose works. We could build an electronic nose that can be even more accurate than a dog's" (Haan 32).

There is still a lot to find out about cancer. Luckily, our best friends are helping us once again.

4. How does the section "Incredible Stories" relate to the central idea of the report?

____

____

____

____

____

____

____

____

5. How does the quotation in the conclusion relate to the central idea?

____

____

____

____

____

____

____

____

6. What is good about the conclusion?

____

____

____

____

____

____

____

____

Name ______________________ Date ____________

Develop a Game Plan

1. Use pages 91–92 to plan your research report. Start by using this diagram to focus your topic and make it specific.

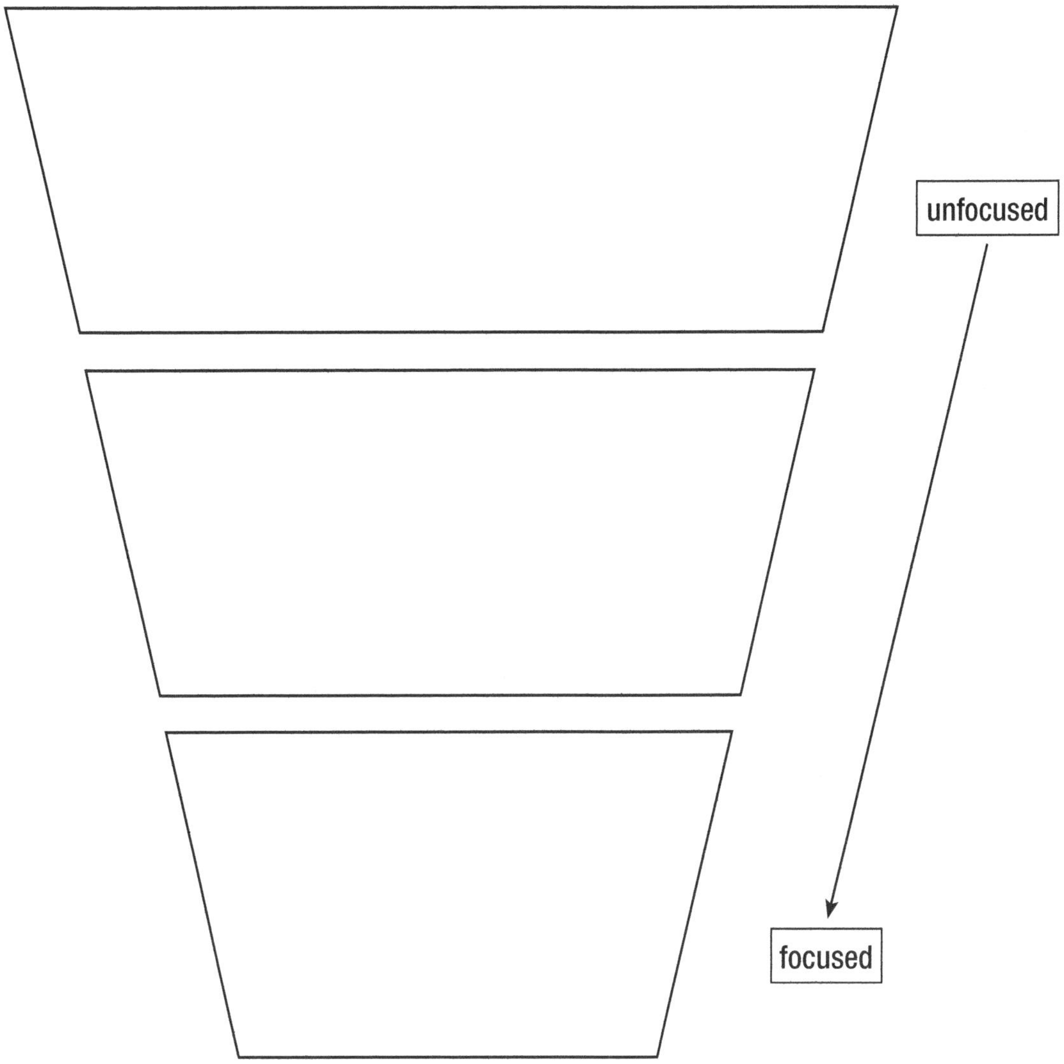

2. Now do a little *presearch* on the Web to get ideas and fine-tune your topic. Then finish filling out your FATP chart.

FATP Chart

Form: *research report*

Audience: *my teacher and classmates*

Topic: ______________________

____

____

Purpose: ______________________

____

____

Develop a Game Plan, continued

3. Now put together some research questions for your report to "answer." Break each question down into more specific sub-questions. Use additional index cards if necessary.

Research Questions

Name ______________________ Date ____________

Locate Information Sources

A. Brainstorm some ideas for the kinds of information sources you could use for your research report. (You can also jot down ideas from direct observation.)

B. Now, list five interview questions you would ask an expert on your topic.

1.

2.

3.

4.

5.

C. Choose three types of published research sources that would be most helpful in your research. Explain why you chose each information source.

Type of Source: ____________________

____

____

Type of Source: ____________________

____

____

Type of Source: ____________________

____

____

D. Use an online catalog to search for print and multimedia resources. List the title (and author, if possible) of each source.

1. ____________________

____

2. ____________________

____

3. ____________________

____

4. ____________________

____

5. ____________________

____

E. List five Web sites that you think will be helpful for writing your research report. Make sure you choose reputable Web sites that you can trust.

1. ____________________

2. ____________________

3. ____________________

4. ____________________

5. ____________________

Name ______________________ Date ____________

Get Information from the Web

A. Spend some time surfing the Web. Look for information about your topic using databases and search engines.

List titles and summaries of three articles you found on databases.

1. ______________________

____

____

____

2. ______________________

____

____

____

3. ______________________

____

____

____

B. List titles and summaries of articles you found through a search engine. If possible, include the Web site address.

1. ______________________

____

____

Web site Address: ______________________

2. ______________________

____

____

Web site Address: ______________________

3. ______________________

____

____

Web site Address: ______________________

Evaluate Sources

Look at these print sources. Then answer the questions.

Recently, great attention has been given to the possibility that dogs use their noses to detect cancer. Many experiments have been made in the United States and in Britain. The results have been encouraging, yet different. Dogs seem to be more reliable in detecting certain kinds of cancers. For examples, dogs detected lung and breast cancer more than 90% of the time. Bladder cancer was recognized only 60% of the time.

—BY MARK SMITH-JONES
from *Riverdale Gazette*, 2014

Dr. Mark Smith-Jones is head of medical services at Lincoln Hospital.

I have always loved dogs, ever since I was a child. We lived on a farm, out in the country, and there were always three or four dogs around the barn and under the porch. Because I grew up with them, I feel I know them very well. I know that dogs can tell how people feel—they get sad when their owners are sad and happy when their owners are happy. And dogs can even tell when their owners are feeling sick—at least my dogs always can!

—BY MARGO ORTEGA
from *Our Canine Friends*, 2010

Margo Ortega is an advocate for animal rights and a best-selling author.

1. Which source is more likely to contain up-to-date information? Why?

____

____

____

____

____

2. Who wrote the material that appears in each print source?

____

____

____

____

3. What is the purpose of each publication? Explain your answer.

____

____

____

____

____

____

____

4. Which source is more likely to be scientifically accurate and reliable? Explain your answer.

____

____

____

____

____

Name ______________________________ Date ______________

Evaluate Sources, continued

Look at the two Web sites. Then answer the questions on page 98.

http://www.dawnscienceproject.com

CLICK HERE to see more pictures of my dog.

CLICK HERE to help me raise money for cancer research!

Dawn's Science Project

March 2014

We all know that dogs are great. If you are lucky to have a dog, then you have a great friend that will never let you down. People have relied on dogs for ages. We used them for gathering sheep and hunting game. We used them for rescuing missing people and leading the blind. Today, dogs are used to improve our health.

Ever heard of pet therapy? In pet therapy, dogs and other animals are used to cheer up people in hopsitals or nursing homes. One of the latest discovery is that dog can be used in cancer reseaerch. Apparently, they can be trained to detect cancer on people. Dogs are really proving to be our best friends, after all!

http://www.westchesteru.edu/sciencetoday

Science Today

Dogs May Be Used to Diagnose Cancer

By Cristina Ferrando, M.D.

Cancer doctors will soon receive some much-needed help. Researchers in California have trained dogs to recognize the scent of cancer cells. Dogs were taught to sit down in front of samples from patients with lung and breast cancer. The dogs guessed correctly up to 97% of the time.

This discovery confirms old tales of dogs sniffing cancerous moles on their owners. It also opens new horizons for cancer research. We all know the advantages of early diagnosis. An early diagnosis often leads to a full recovery. Dogs seem to detect cancer at a very early stage.

Last updated: May 17, 2014

1. What is the purpose of each site? Explain your answer.

2. Who wrote the material that appears on each site?

3. Which of the two Web sites is more likely to contain up-to-date information? Why?

4. Based on the two sites' URLs, which site is more reliable? Why?

5. Which of the two Web sites looks more professional? Explain your answer.

6. Would you use the first Web site as a source for a report on dogs and medicine? Why or why not?

Name ______________________ Date ______________

Locate Relevant Information

Skim this magazine article. Then answer the questions.

Friendly Paws

A new association has recently opened in our community. Friendly Paws is a nonprofit association that brings therapy dogs to people in need. People in nursing homes, hospitals, and schools will benefit from the therapeutic company of a dog.

What Is a Therapy Dog?

Dogs always have the power to cheer us up. This is the simple idea behind canine therapy. In fact, scientific research has shown that dogs can greatly improve a person's mental well-being. A therapy dog is a dog trained to comfort people in need. Therapy dogs are mostly used with the elderly and people struggling with illness. A therapy dog has a nice character and is never aggressive. It can help people feel calmer and happier.

Dog Handlers at Friendly Paws

Most of the dog handlers from Friendly Paws have worked in animal shelters. Others have studied canine behavior. Others still are psychotherapists. These dog handlers can assign the perfect therapy dog to each person. A young and lively puppy provides a very different therapy than an older, calmer dog. Friendly Paws knows, however, that both dogs are invaluable companions.

1. What do the title and beginning sentences tell you about the article's topic?

2. Which information in this article could be useful to someone writing about dogs employed in the diagnosis of cancer? Why?

3. Which information in this article is not relevant to a report about dogs and cancer research?

Take Good Notes

Practice Using Note Cards

Study the note card. Then answer the questions.

Gila Monsters—Physical characteristics

— 16 inches long
— short, blunt head
— coloring is black, brown, or orange
— come out only at night during summer and during the day in winter
— eat bird and reptile eggs
— fat tail (where it stores fat)
— move very slowly

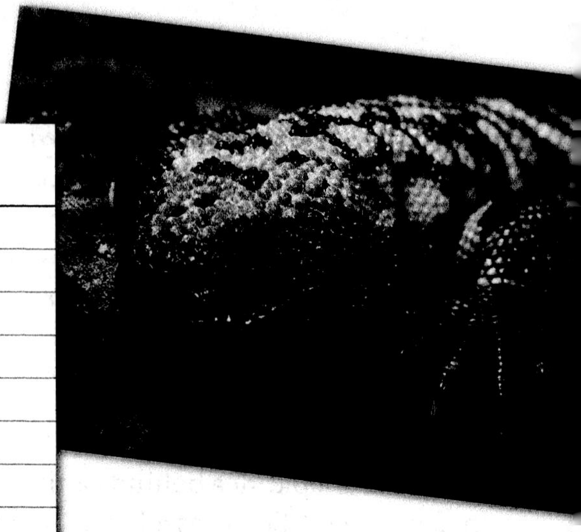

1. Is the heading on this note card appropriate? Explain your answer.

2. What could you do to better organize the information?

3. What is missing from the note card?

Name ____________________ Date ____________

Take Good Notes, continued

Read the excerpt. Then take notes on the index card. Don't forget to include a heading and a source note.

from *The Bite of the Komodo Dragon* by Graham Farris

41

The Komodo dragon is one of the scariest animals on our planet. The Komodo dragon is a big, strong lizard. It can be up to 10 feet long.

Komodo dragons have a peculiar characteristic. Their saliva contains lethal bacteria. So, if an animal is bitten by a Komodo dragon, it will die soon after because of the reptile's bite.

Scientists are very interested in the Komodo dragon's saliva. They wonder how these animals can be immune to the deadly bacteria in their mouths.

Scientists think the Komodo dragon has special antibodies. (Antibodies are molecules that destroy bacteria in living beings.) Studying the antibodies in the Komodo dragon can help scientists create powerful medicine for humans.

Practice Paraphrasing

Read each passage.
Then paraphrase the important ideas.

Studying the Komodo Dragon
By Darryl McKinney

Recently, scientists have shown interest in the Komodo dragon. They want to study the lizard's ability to survive its own poisonous saliva. In order to do this, they must collect samples from a live animal. This is not an easy task. Usually, rangers use a lasso and ropes to immobilize the Komodo dragon. They must be extremely careful. The Komodo dragon is incredibly strong and fast.

The Strongest Lizard
By Dr. Lawrence Mishkin

The Komodo dragon takes its name from the Komodo Island, in the south of the Indian Ocean. It is there that most Komodo dragons live.

The Komodo dragon is very big in size. It can be up to 10 feet long and can weigh over 300 pounds. The Komodo dragon is a skilled predator. Despite its weight, it is extremely fast and agile. Its strong jaws, lined with about 60 razor-sharp teeth, can kill prey as big as a water buffalo.

At a Glance

To paraphrase:

- read the source carefully
- record the important information in your own words
- keep your paraphrase about the same length as the original text or a bit shorter.

Practice Summarizing

1. Read the article carefully. Then summarize it.

Diagnosing Cancer with Dogs: The Experiment

By Kathy Lopez

The news that dogs might be able to detect cancer has spread around the world. The discovery came thanks to an experiment at the Pine Street Foundation of San Anselmo, California. But how was the experiment conducted?

The researchers chose five dogs. There were male and female dogs. All of them were under 18 months and had been trained for obedience. First the dogs were trained to recognize breath samples provided by cancer patients. Then the dogs were tested with a mix of samples provided by 55 lung-cancer patients, 31 breast-cancer patients, and 83 healthy people.

The dogs were 99% accurate identifying the lung-cancer cases. They were 88% accurate with the breast-cancer cases. False positives—misidentifying a healthy person as having cancer—were 2% or less!

At a Glance

To summarize:

- read the source carefully
- keep track of important ideas and details
- restate the main idea in your own words
- include only the important details and examples
- check for accuracy.

Main Idea:

____

____

____

____

Summary:

____

____

____

____

____

____

____

____

____

____

2. Now take notes on the sources you have decided to use for your information report. Paraphrase and summarize as needed. Don't forget to include headings and to record the sources.

Avoid Plagiarism

Read the source and the student report. Then edit the student report to fix any plagiarism.

At a Glance

To avoid accidental plagiarism:

- use quotation marks around any text taken directly from a source
- use your own wording and sentence patterns when paraphrasing ideas
- give credit to the writer (or source) whenever you quote or paraphrase another writer's ideas.

Source

Unexpected Properties of Snake Venom

By Lili J. Rubin

The venom of poisonous snakes is under scrutiny today. That is because snake venom could improve our health. A few years ago, the venom of a Brazilian snake was used in a medicine that lowered blood pressure.

Today, researchers are focusing on the venom of another species of snake. This venom could be used to treat cancer.

It seems that the venom could destroy cancer cells. What is even more surprising is that it would do so without damaging the healthy cells around it.

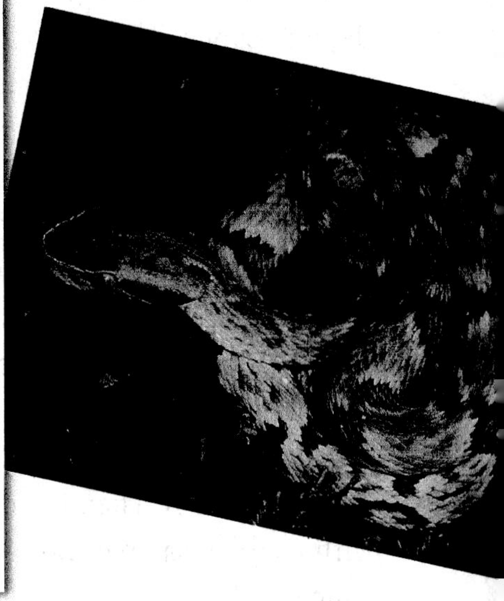

Student Paper

Snake Venom and Medicine

Today, the venom of poisonous snakes is under scrutiny. That's because snake venom could actually be beneficial to our health. In fact, a few years ago, the venom of a Brazilian snake was used in medicine that lowered blood pressure.

Researchers are now studying the venom of another type of snake. They hope that this venom will be used in the fight against cancer. The hope is that this venom could destroy cancer cells. What is even more important, it would do so without damaging the healthy cells around it.

Name ______________________ Date ______________

Using Direct Quotes

1. On each index card, record an important quote from the article. Use ellipses or brackets as needed.

The Strength of Spider Webs

by Miriam P. Elder

Spider webs are truly a marvel of nature. They are delicately spun and look beautiful. However, they have other characteristics that attract scientists' attention. A spider web is incredibly resistant and elastic. It is actually proven that spider silk is, by weight, stronger than steel.

Spider silk could have many uses in medicine. It could be used to bond together broken ligaments. It could be used as thread for stitches.

It is unlikely that hospitals around the world will start breeding spiders. It would take too many spiders to produce a usable amount of spider silk. So scientists are trying to reproduce spider silk in a laboratory. They hope they can soon create a similar fiber that is strong, elastic, and biodegradable.

14

At a Glance

Follow these tips when you use a direct quote:

- copy the words exactly
- use brackets [ ] around any words you changed
- use ellipses (...) to show where you left words out.

Spider Webs—Characteristics

"A spider web is incredibly resistant and elastic."

Elder, 14

2. Record one good quote you plan to use in your research report.

Organize Your Notes

Practice Synthesizing Ideas

Study the Inquiry Chart. Then write a synthesis of the information presented for each research question.

Research Questions	Source Information	Synthesis
What are the latest discoveries in the field of medicine that involve animals?	Dogs can be trained to sniff various kinds of cancer in people. (Lewis 12) The saliva of Komodo dragons is being studied for its resistance to powerful and deadly bacteria. (Epstein 60) Researchers are trying to recreate the strength and flexibility of spider silk to create artificial tendons and resistant stitches. (Klatz 32)	
How could the latest discoveries affect our health?	Diagnosis of cancer is becoming more accurate and reliable with the use of trained dogs. (Romero 34) The antibodies of the Komodo dragon could be used to develop medicines against strong bacteria and virus strains. (Molina 101) It might take a few years before scientists unlock the secrets of certain animal characteristics and employ them in medicine. (Lovgren 11)	

Name ______________________ Date ______________

Organize Your Notes, continued

Check for Focus

Delete any information that doesn't relate to the research question. Then write a synthesis of the information.

Research Questions	Source Information	Synthesis
How can maggots be used in medicine?	Maggots eat bacteria in open wounds, helping the healing process. (Simmons 5) Serious wounds are treated with surgical operations. (Cooper 33) Patients treated with maggots do not feel any pain during the treatment. (Klatz 32) Maggots turn into larvae and finally into flies. (Richardson 27) The Food and Drug Administration has approved the use of maggots as medical treatment. (Caron 61) Maggots have been used successfully to treat infected wounds, serious burns, and even skin cancer. (Turner 83)	

Develop an Outline

1. Write a draft of your outline for your research report:

- use roman numerals for the main topics in your paper
- use capital letters for ideas that will become the main ideas in your paragraphs
- use numbers for details.

Name ______________________________ Date ______________

Develop an Outline, continued

2. Now type your outline with correct indentation and paste it here.

Draft a Research Report

1. Use the outline to draft an introductory paragraph for this report.

I. Introduction – Help from a dangerous predator

A. venom from cone snails can paralyze and kill fish or humans

B. a molecule in the venom can help relieve pain in humans

C. scientists have worked for years trying to separate the molecule from the venom

2. Now use your outline from pages 108–109 to draft the introductory paragraph for your research report.

Name ______________________ Date ____________

Draft a Research Report, continued

3. Use the outline to draft a body paragraph for this report.

II. How the venom works

A. snail has a venomous stinger that shoots out of its mouth

B. a chemical in the venom stops pain signals from going to the brain

4. Now use your outline from pages 108–109 to draft a body paragraph for your research report.

5. Use the outline to draft a concluding paragraph for this report.

V. Conclusion

A. research has led to the creation of a new medicine, Ziconotide

B. for people with cancer or other serious diseases

C. not addictive, unlike many other painkillers

6. Now use your outline from pages 108–109 to draft the conclusion for your research report.

Name ______________________ Date ______________

Practice Citing Sources

Use the source cards to create entries for a "Works Cited" page. (See pages 198W–199W in your Writing book for guidelines on formatting entries for different kinds of sources.)

Source #1
Type: Book
Title: New Treatments for Cancer
Author: Melinda T. Jackson
Publisher: Embry Press
City: Chicago
Year: 2013

Source #2
Type: Interview
Format: MP3
Interviewer: Alan Samoska
Name: Samuel Mills, M.D.
Location: St. Luke's Hospital, St. Louis
Date: April 9, 2014

Source #3
Type: Magazine article
Article title: "Cancer-Fighting Proteins in Chicken Eggs"
Magazine title: Pharmacy Monthly
Author: Rosanna M. Sanchez, M.D.
Pages: 17–23
Month: May
Year: 2007

Works Cited

1. ______________________________

2. ______________________________

3. ______________________________

Create a List of Works Cited

Create a list of works cited for your research report.
Include all the sources that provided information in your final report.

Works Cited

Name ______________________________ Date ______________

Revise a Research Report

1. Use the checklist. Evaluate this draft of the beginning of a research report on the medical uses of cone-snail venom. What changes are needed?

____

____

____

____

____

Revising Checklist

- ❑ Do you need to add more details to make your central idea more specific?
- ❑ Do you need to take out any information that is not related to the central idea?
- ❑ Do you need to move any sentences to improve the flow of ideas?

2. Revise the draft. Use revising marks to show your changes.

Revising

MARK	WHAT IT MEANS
∧	Insert something.
↶○	Move to here.
⌐	Replace with this.
⌒ℓ	Take out.
¶	Make a new paragraph.

A Poisonous Pain Reliever

If you're ever swimming and see a cone snail, swim away from it. Cone snails' venom can paralyze and kill other animals (Kamali 34). Cone snail shells can have bright patterns.

Scientists who analyzed cone-snail venom for over 20 years made an amazing discovery (Lee 91). The venom can be harmful to humans, too. Small doses of it can relieve pain. Scientists used it to create a new medication. This medication is used to treat people suffering from chronic pain or terminal diseases (Wong 57).

3. Now use the checklist to help you revise the draft of your research report.

Edit and Proofread

Grammar Workout: Check Possessive Adjectives

Choose the correct word to complete each sentence.

1. Once, ____________ dad was stung by three bees.
me/my

2. When bees sting, it is often to defend ____________ beehive.
they/their

3. After it stings, a honey bee loses ____________ stinger and dies.
its/it

4. Make sure that there are no beehives close to ____________ home.
your/you

5. ____________ house is next to a farm.
Us/Our

6. The farmer uses bees to pollinate ____________ trees.
he's/his

Spelling Workout: Check Spelling of Long Words

Find the spelling error in each of the following words.
Rewrite the word correctly.

1. atnibodies ____________

2. dianosing ____________

3. thretening ____________

4. hybernated ____________

5. tenatiously ____________

6. hachlings ____________

Name ______________________ Date ______________

Edit and Proofread, continued

Mechanics Workout: Check Apostrophes in Possessive Nouns

Rewrite the underlined phrase using a possessive noun.

1. The saliva of the Gila monster is used in medicine. The Gila monster's saliva
2. The interest of the medical community is high. ______________________
3. Not all the bites by snakes are venomous. ______________________
4. The contribution of animals to medicine is relevant. ______________________
5. The report written by Mike Lewis is interesting. ______________________

Check Grammar, Spelling, and Mechanics

Proofread the passage. Check the spelling and the use of possessive adjectives and apostrophes. Correct the mistakes.

Editing and Proofreading Marks

^	Insert something.
^ with comma	Add a comma.
^ with semicolon	Add a semicolon.
⊙	Add a period.
⊙ with colon	Add a colon.
∨ with quotation marks	Add quotation marks.
∨ with apostrophe	Add an apostrophe.
≡	Capitalize.
/	Make lowercase.
℘	Delete.
¶	Make new paragraph.
⬭	Check spelling.
‸ with line	Replace with this.
∽	Change order.
#	Insert space.
⁐	Close up.

Snakes are not the only dangerous animals studied in medicine. Reseaerchers today are studying Komodo dragons saliva. This animals saliva is rich in harmful bactera. Scientists must capture a Komodo dragon alive and collect samples of it's saliva. Often, researchers use a lasso. They also need to make sure these prehystoric predaters don't bite them hands. These reptile's mouths are lined with very sharp teeth. If a Komodo dragon decides you will be it prey, there is little you can do. A scientist life is very adventuruos today!

Edit and Proofread Your Research Report

Now edit and proofread your work.

1. Use a checklist as you edit and proofread. Add things you are working on to the checklist.

2. Look to see which errors are marked most often. Jot down your top three trouble spots.

____

____

____

Remember to Check

- [ ] possessive adjectives
- [ ] spelling of long words
- [ ] apostrophes in possessive nouns
- [ ] ____________
- [ ] ____________

3. Ask your teacher about ways to fix these mistakes, or check out the Grammar Handbook for information.

Focus on Spelling

Improve your spelling by following these steps.

1. Create a personal spelling list. Record words that you misspelled. Look up correct spelling in the dictionary and add these words to **My Spelling List.**

2. Pick twelve words. Focus on four words each day. Write your words before each meal and check the spelling. At the end of the week, try writing all twelve words.

3. Have a partner stand with his or her back to the board. List your partner's spelling words on the board. Say each word and ask your partner to spell it. Then switch roles.

4. Organize your words into lists. List them from shortest word to longest word. Next list them from easiest to hardest. Try listing them in reverse alphabetical order.

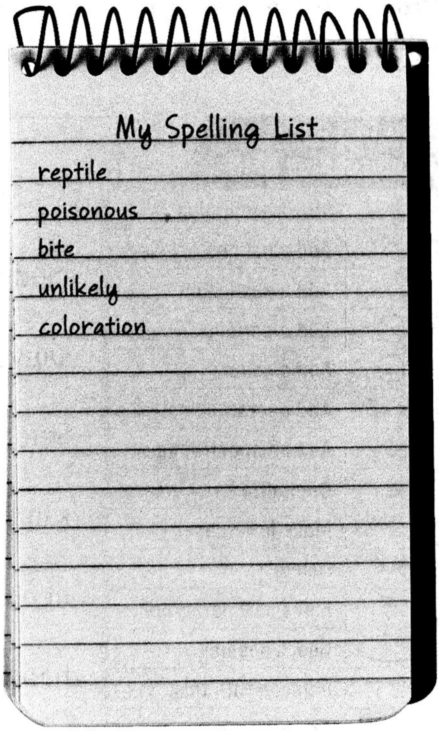

5. Invent your own acronyms. Think of a word that begins with each letter. The words in the correct order should be easy for you to remember. For example:

Spelling word	Acronym
ocean	octopus, coral, eel are near

Name ______________________ Date ____________

Publish, Share, and Reflect

Publish and Share Your Research Report

Check the final formats you used to publish your research report. Then answer the following questions.

Publishing

What was the final format of your project?	How did you share your project?
☐ Wrote it neatly by hand	☐ Shared it with a large group
☐ Typed it on a computer	☐ Shared it with a small group

1. Whether you published it by hand or on the computer, what did you do to dress up your final project?

____

____

____

____

____

2. How did you share your work? What did you learn through sharing your work?

____

____

____

____

____

____

____

____

____

____

____

____

____

Reflect on Your Research

Reflect on the process you used to research and write your report.

Write the title of your report here: ______________________________

Gathering Information

1. What did you do that helped you gather information for your report?

____

____

2. What will you do differently when you gather information for your next report?

____

____

Organizing and Digesting Information

3. What did you do that helped you organize and digest information for your report?

____

____

____

4. What will you do differently when you organize and digest information for your next report?

____

____

Presenting Information

5. What did you do that helped you present information in your report?

____

____

6. What will you do differently when you present information in your next report?

____

____

Name ____________________ Date ____________

Analyze a Story Scene

What makes this story scene a good model? Read the story scene and answer the questions.

The Ship's Port

by David Romero

A noisy crowd of people was waiting around the Southside Seaport—a favorite stop of sailors from around the world. Some people were waiting to board a ferry. Their frantic calls meant to keep their children in line were heard in several languages. Others, just stepping off ships, spoke in quiet tones. The sounds and dialects mingled together to create a melody heard nowhere else. Whether one was coming or going, an exciting feeling always hung over the port.

Red, yellow, and blue umbrella carts competed with the tourists and sailors for the best spaces. To a sailor who had been surviving on stale bread and fish, these carts were a welcome sight! The carts were filled with roasted nuts, hot dogs, sausages, and cabbage. Their sweet and spicy smells filled the air. Lines of hungry sailors formed around the tiny cafes. Once their bellies were full, the sailors ventured into the city.

Soon leave was over and it was time to reboard the ship. Passing through the iron arches of the port, the sailors took a last look around. They'd remember fondly their full bellies and the time they spent walking on steady ground.

Feature Checklist

A good story scene

- ☐ helps readers imagine something that has happened
- ☐ uses vivid and precise language to tell where and when the action takes place
- ☐ includes sensory details to describe the events.

1. What vivid and precise language does the writer use?

____

____

____

____

____

____

2. What senses does the writer's story scene appeal to? Give examples.

____

____

____

____

____

____

____

3. How does the writer help you imagine being at a port?

____

____

____

____

____

____

Plan a Story Scene

Use this page to plan your story scene.

1. List a few ideas for a topic. Then choose the best one.

Ideas	Good Topic for a Story Scene?

2. Get clear on your audience and purpose. Complete an FATP chart for your story scene.

FATP Chart

Form: ______________________

Audience: ______________________

Topic: ______________________

Purpose: ______________________

____

3. Gather the details for your story scene. Complete a five-senses diagram.

I saw . . .	
I heard . . .	
I smelled . . .	
I tasted . . .	
I touched or felt . . .	

Five-Senses Diagram

Name ______________________ Date ______________

Draft a Story Scene

Use your plan from page 122 to write the first draft of your story scene.

Drafting Checklist

- ☐ Grab your readers' interest right away.
- ☐ Help readers imagine something that has happened.
- ☐ Use vivid and precise language to tell where and when the action takes place.
- ☐ Add plenty of sensory details.

Revise a Story Scene

1. Use the checklist to evaluate this draft of a story scene. What changes are needed?

____

____

____

____

____

Revising Checklist

- ☐ Do you need to add any information or sensory details to make the story scene clearer?
- ☐ Are there any unimportant details that can be removed?
- ☐ Should you move any sentences to improve the flow of ideas?

2. Revise the draft. Use revising marks to show your changes.

Revising

MARK	WHAT IT MEANS
∧	Insert something.
(loop with arrow)	Move to here.
(replace mark)	Replace with this.
(take-out mark)	Take out.
¶	Make a new paragraph.

The Bow and Arrow

The bow and arrow was an important tool to Native Americans. It was used for both hunting and defense. The bow was made with a long piece of wood. A length of string connected the ends, bending the bow into the shape of the letter "D."

The arrow was made from a piece of wood. One end, called the tail, held feathers. The other end held an object called an arrowhead. Native Americans shaped their arrowheads out of hard materials. An arrow could move quickly through the air and hit a target accurately.

3. Now use the checklist to help you revise the draft of your story scene on page 123.

Name ______________________ Date ____________

Edit and Proofread

Grammar Workout: Check Frequently Misused Verbs

Choose the correct verb to complete each sentence.

1. I had to **(lay/lie)** __________ down the mixing spoon for just a second.

2. When I went to **(sit/set)** __________ the bowl on the counter, it fell on the floor.

3. I finally got the cake in the oven, but it didn't **(raise/ rise)** __________.

4. I told my guests to **(sit/set)** __________ down at the table.

5. "Will anyone who wants flat cake please **(raise/rise)** __________ his or her hand?" I asked.

Spelling Workout: Check Suffixes

Add the suffix *–ful* to these words:

1. beauty __________

2. bounty __________

3. plenty __________

4. spite __________

5. duty __________

6. use __________

Add the suffix *–ness* or *–less* to these words:

7. crazy __________

8. happy __________

9. grouchy __________

10. cozy __________

11. mercy __________

12. pity __________

Add the suffix *–y* to these words:

13. spice __________

14. juice __________

15. shine __________

16. haze __________

17. able __________

18. ache __________

Mechanics Workout: Check Serial Commas

Insert commas in the sentences below to make each meaning clear.

1. Wojapi, a classic Plains Indian pudding, is made with blueberries, raspberries and cherries.

2. It is warm creamy and sweet.

3. Amelia Adam, and Jordan had several helpings.

4. Mrs. Griggs Shawn and I did not even get to taste it before it was gone.

Check Grammar, Spelling, and Mechanics

Proofread the passage. Check the spelling and the use of frequently misused verbs and serial commas.

Editing and Proofreading Marks

Mark	Meaning
^	Insert something.
^ with comma	Add a comma.
^ with semicolon	Add a semicolon.
⊙	Add a period.
⊙ with colon	Add a colon.
˅ with quotation marks	Add quotation marks.
˅ with apostrophe	Add an apostrophe.
≡	Capitalize.
/	Make lowercase.
℘	Delete.
¶	Make new paragraph.
⬭	Check spelling.
⌃ with line	Replace with this.
∽	Change order.
#	Insert space.
⁀‿	Close up.

Mrs. Robinson's class sit out a Native American feast. Everyone agreed it was wonderfull. It was a way to learn about another culture. The food facts and fun of the afternoon helped to rise the students' appreciation of what they are learning in social studies class. They especialy enjoyed the warm hearty and creamy stew. And they couldn't get enough of the tastey fry bread. The fluffiness and sweetness of the pastry made their mouths water. Luckily, everyone could have seconds because the bread was so plentyiful.

Edit and Proofread Your Story Scene

Now edit and proofread your work.

Remember to Check

- ❑ frequently misused verbs
- ❑ spelling of words with suffixes
- ❑ serial commas
- ❑ ______________
- ❑ ______________

1. Use a checklist as you edit and proofread. Add things you are working on to the checklist.

2. Look to see which errors are marked most often. Jot down your top three trouble spots.

____

____

____

3. Ask your teacher about ways to fix these mistakes, or check out the Grammar Handbook for information.

Focus on Spelling

Improve your spelling by following these steps.

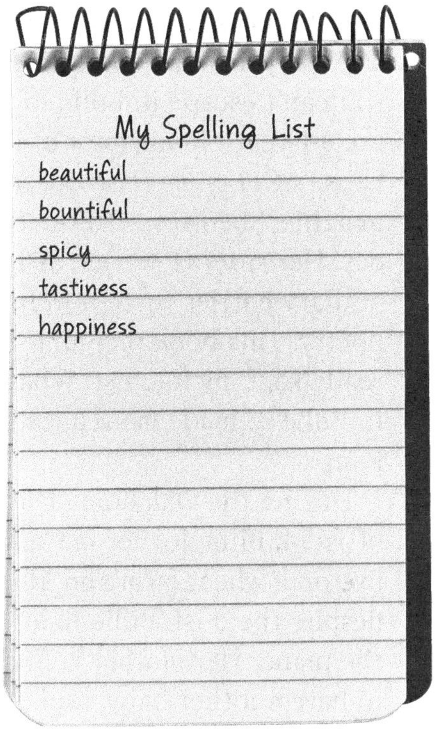

1. Create a personal spelling list. Record words that you misspelled. Look up correct spelling in the dictionary and add these words to **My Spelling List**.

2. Pick twelve words. Make a colorful display of the words. Get a sheet of chart paper. Write each word three times in a different color.

3. Work with a partner to play **Spelling Tic-Tac-Toe**. Draw a tic-tac-toe board. Take turns asking each other to spell words. When a player spells a word correctly, that player gets to mark an X or an O on the game board. The game continues until one player is able to draw a vertical, diagonal, or horizontal line through the X's or O's.

4. Write the letters for each word on separate squares of paper. Attach the letters for each word to each other with a paper clip. Unscramble the letters to spell each of your words.

5. Invent your own memory strategy for difficult words. Think of a good way to remember *why* letters appear in a word or not. For example:

Word	Explanation
dessert	"It has two s's for sweet stuff!"

Analyze a Literary Response

What makes this literary response a good model? Read the literary response and answer the questions.

Feature Checklist

A good literary response

- ❏ quickly summarizes what you read
- ❏ states your ideas and claims about the literature
- ❏ expresses your personal response to the literature
- ❏ uses evidence from the text to support your opinions
- ❏ may mention what you learned from the text.

Out of the Dust

by Karen Hesse

Reviewed by Naomi Watkins

Imagine the taste of dust in your mouth, the feel of it in your hair, the smell of it in your nose. Imagine that you can't escape it. Billie Jo Kelby, the 14-year-old narrator of Karen Hesse's *Out of the Dust*, doesn't have to imagine. She lives with the dust every day. Her story is written as a series of diary entries written in free-form poetry. This book is so unusual that it really kept my interest. What happened to Billie Jo made me realize how lucky I am.

During the Oklahoma Dust Bowl of 1934, Billie Jo, her ma, and her pa live on a wheat farm and are happy, despite the dust. Billie Jo loves to play the piano. Her mother is finally going to have another baby. And her father is optimistic about the rain coming. But a terrible accident changes everything. Ma mistakes the kerosene Pa put next to the stove for water. The resulting fire kills Ma and the baby. Billie Jo's hands are terribly burned. Her pa becomes depressed. Billie Jo wants to make things better, but can't.

1. What does the reviewer say *Out of the Dust* is mostly about?

____

____

____

____

____

____

____

____

____

____

2. What is the writer's overall opinion about the book?

____

____

____

____

____

____

____

____

____

____

Analyze a Literary Response, continued

This book is really about finding out who you are and how you became that person. Billie Jo is consumed by her guilt. She is also blinded by anger at her pa. She tries to get away on a freight train. The farther away she goes, the more she starts to understand her pa. She says, "My father stayed rooted," and "even with my tests and my temper, even with the double sorrow of his grief and my own, he had kept a home until I broke it." So, she returns home to her father. And she tells him she has learned she can't really leave. She says, "I tell him about getting out of the dust and how I can't get out of something that's inside of me." She also remarks, "I know that all the time I was trying to get out of the dust, the fact is, what I am, I am because of the dust."

I have never had a parent die or leave home. But I have stormed out of a room after having a fight with my mom and dad. And as crazy as it sounds, all I ever want to do is go back in there. I realize that the thing I need most is really what I have left behind. Family makes you who and what you are. That's because no one loves, or forgives you, like family.

3. What evidence from the book does the writer use to support her opinion about the book's message?

4. How does the writer sum up her feelings about the book?

5. What has the writer learned from reading the book?

Evaluate for Development of Ideas

Read each literary response. Use the rubric on page 131 to score each response for development of ideas. Explain your scores.

Writing Sample 1

The Cay

by Theodore Taylor

Reviewed by Shawn Merris

Theodore Taylor's *The Cay* is the best book I've read in a long time. It is a moving story about a friendship that develops between two strangers.

The story is about a young boy, Phillip, who lives on the island of Curacao at the start of World War II. He and his mom try to escape the war, but their ship is sunk. Phillip is left floating on a wooden raft. So is Timothy, an old black man from the West Indies. Phillip has been blinded.

The two drift ashore. Phillip doesn't like Timothy at first. He has been influenced by his mom's prejudice. But Timothy teaches Phillip how to survive despite his blindness, and Phillip's attitude changes.

This story made me think a lot about relationships. It reminded me that you should always look for who someone is on the inside.

Score	1	2	3	4

Writing Sample 2

The Cay

by Theodore Taylor

Reviewed by Kirsten Eklund

The Cay is a good book. I liked it.

Phillip and his mom try to escape during World War II, but their ship sinks. Phillip and a black man named Timothy survive. Phillip is blind.

The two float on a raft until they reach the shore. Phillip doesn't like Timothy. Then Timothy teaches Phillip how to survive. This story made me think about friendship. Your friends can teach you a lot.

Score	1	2	3	4

Name ______________________ Date ______________

Evaluate for Development of Ideas, continued

Writing Rubric

Development of Ideas		
	How thoughtful and interesting is the writing?	How well are the ideas or claims explained and supported?
4 **Wow!**	The writing engages the reader with meaningful ideas or claims and presents them in a way that is interesting and appropriate to the audience, purpose, and type of writing.	**The ideas or claims are fully explained and supported.** • The ideas or claims are well developed with important details, evidence, and/or description. • The writing feels complete, and the reader is satisfied.
3 **Ahh.**	Most of the writing engages the reader with meaningful ideas or claims and presents them in a way that is interesting and appropriate to the audience, purpose, and type of writing.	**Most of the ideas or claims are explained and supported.** • Most of the ideas or claims are developed with important details, evidence, and/or description. • The writing feels mostly complete, but the reader still has some questions.
2 **Hmm.**	Some of the writing engages the reader with meaningful ideas or claims and presents them in a way that is interesting and appropriate to the audience, purpose, and type of writing.	**Some of the ideas or claims are explained and supported.** • Only some of the ideas or claims are developed. Details, evidence, and/or description, are limited or not relevant. • The writing leaves the reader with many questions.
1 **Huh?**	The writing does not engage the reader. It is not appropriate to the audience, purpose, and type of writing.	**The ideas or claims are not explained or supported.** The ideas lack details, evidence, and/or description, and the writing leaves the reader unsatisfied.

Raise the Score

1. Use the rubric on page 131 to evaluate and score this literary response.

Score	1	2	3	4

Culture Clash

by Peter Winkler and Fran Downey

Reviewed by Selena Acosta

The authors of this article tell about the Aztec. They explain how the Spanish defeated them. I liked learning how this happened.

In 1519, Spanish explorers arrived in the Aztec capital city of Tenochtitlán. They liked the city. It was an amazing city. They'd never seen a city so beautiful. The Spanish wanted to take over Tenochtitlán. They wanted the rest of Mexico. So they started a war. For two years they fought the large Aztec army. But weapons didn't defeat the Aztec. It was a virus. The virus made the Aztec sick so they couldn't farm. It killed a lot of them. The Spanish finally won.

One part tells how the Spanish and Mexican cultures eventually blended. Some things became both Spanish and Mexican.

Culture Clash is a good article. Everyone should read it.

2. Explain what the writer should do to raise the score:

Name ______________________ Date ______________

Raise the Score, continued

3. Now revise the literary response on page 132 to improve the development of ideas. Write your revised response here.

Write Good Beginnings

Read the paragraph. Write some new beginning sentences for the paragraph that will do a better job of grabbing the reader's interest.

Julia Alvarez's book *Before We Were Free* is very interesting. *Before We Were Free* tells the story of Anita de la Torre. Anita escaped from a dictatorship in the Dominican Republic when she was a child. In the book, Anita and her family struggle to stay alive. This book paints a realistic picture of one family's fight for freedom.

1. Use a thought-provoking question.

____

____

____

2. Give an interesting statistic.

____

____

____

3. Start with a quotation.

____

____

____

4. Begin with a personal connection.

____

____

____

Name ______________________ Date ______________

Write Good Endings

Read the paragraphs from a literary response. Write a good ending that summarizes the writer's ideas.

Steps to Summarize

- ❑ Read the paper carefully.
- ❑ Restate the main ideas.
- ❑ Condense important details.

Before We Were Free

by Julia Alvarez

Reviewed by Anthony Gravina

What would your life be like if you had to go into hiding from the government? What would you do to be free? These are the questions that Anita de la Torre must face in *Before We Were Free*. This book describes Anita's experience in the Dominican Republic. It taught me about part of the history of the Dominican Republic. The book also caught my interest because it featured a brave main character and an exciting plot.

When the secret police arrest Anita's family members, Anita and her mother go into hiding. During this time, Anita keeps a diary of her experiences. Eventually, Anita and her mother are rescued and taken to the United States. Many of Anita's family members, however, are gone forever.

Reading Anita's diary entries made me feel like I was hiding right along with her. Before reading this book, I didn't know much about the history of the Dominican Republic. Now, though, I feel like I've experienced life under a dictatorship through Anita's eyes.

Read the weak ending of a literary response about *Before We Were Free*. Use techniques for finishing strong to rewrite the ending.

> Anita has typical 12-year-old problems and emotions. But she has to go through some very hard things, too. I liked reading about how she handled herself during the revolution.

1. End with a question.

2. End with a personal experience.

3. End with a quotation.

Name ______________________ Date ______________

Explain and Support Your Ideas

Read the paragraph from a literary response about the short story "Encounter." Follow the directions to improve the paragraph.

> "Encounter," by Jane Yolen, is a story about a wise boy. The boy's dreams come true. He tries to warn his people of danger, but they do not believe him. The story has a sad ending that really made me think.

1. Write down facts and details from the story that could be included in this paragraph.

____

____

____

____

____

____

2. Write down examples of evidence from the story that support the paragraph's ideas.

____

____

____

____

____

____

3. Write down direct quotations from the story that support the ideas and examples.

____

____

____

____

____

____

4. Write down your own thoughts about the story.

5. Use the facts, details, examples, quotations, and thoughts you gathered in steps 1–4 to write a new version of the paragraph. Make sure to explain and support your ideas with evidence from the story.

Name ______________________ Date ______________

Plan a Literary Response

Use pages 139–140 to plan your literary response.

1. List a few books; then choose the one that means the most to you.

2. Reread or review your book. Summarize all the important ideas in the chart.

Book
Thoughts and reactions
What's good about it?
Would I recommend this work to other people? Why or why not?

3. Gather and organize support for your opinions. Use an opinion chart.

OPINIONS	SUPPORTING EVIDENCE

Name ______________________ Date ____________

Draft a Literary Response

Use your plan from pages 139–140 to write the first draft of your literary response.

Drafting Checklist

- ☐ Quickly summarize what you have read.
- ☐ State your ideas and claims about the merits of the literature.
- ☐ Express your opinions and your personal response to the literature.
- ☐ Use evidence and examples from the text to support your opinions.
- ☐ Try to mention something that you learned from reading the text.

Name ____________________ Date __________

Revise a Literary Response

1. Use the checklist to evaluate this draft of a literary response. What changes are needed?

____

____

____

____

____

____

Revising Checklist

- ☐ Is there a summary of what you read?
- ☐ Is there a personal response to the work?
- ☐ Is there enough evidence from the text to support the ideas and opinions?
- ☐ Would a reader have any unanswered questions?

2. Revise this draft. Use revising marks to show your changes.

Revising

MARK	WHAT IT MEANS
∧	Insert something.
(move mark)	Move to here.
(replace mark)	Replace with this.
(delete mark)	Take out.
¶	Make a new paragraph.

Alone in the Wilderness

by Hap Gilliland

Reviewed by Peter Takahashi

Could you imagine living alone in the wilds of Montana for three months? That's what a resourceful teenager named Flint Red Coyote does in Hap Gilliland's book *Alone in the Wilderness*. As a minority, Flint encounters racial discrimination from his fellow students. I could relate to Flint's character.

Flint sets out on a three-month journey. It's very hard to live alone in the wilderness. He prepares himself with the help of his Cheyenne elders.

3. Now use the checklist to help you revise the draft of your literary response on pages 141–142.

Edit and Proofread

Grammar Workout: Check Past Tense Verbs

Write the correct past tense form of each verb in parentheses.

1. After I read Ned's story, I ____________ it would be neat to talk in code. **(think)**

2. I ____________ my friends about his job as a code talker. **(tell)**

3. We got together and ____________ our own code. **(write)**

4. It was really fun to send notes that no one but us ____________ how to read! **(know)**

5. I wish I could thank the code talkers for the great idea they ____________ us! **(give)**

Spelling Workout: Check Verbs with Endings

Find and fix the spelling mistake in each sentence.

1. The code talkers createed a system of Navajo words to represent the letters of the English alphabet.

2. They made more code by nameing U.S. military terms with their own expressions, like "iron-fish" for "submarine."

3. The code talkers spent many hours puting the military's messages into the new code.

4. The military prefered to have its agents memorize the secret code.

5. That way, no printed materials about the code could be captureed.

Edit and Proofread, continued

Mechanics Workout: Check Titles of Literary Works

Correctly punctuate the title of each literary work.

1. I lent Joseph Bruchac's book Code Talkers to my friend Amy.
2. Amy went online and found an essay titled The Codes of World War II by John Shepler.
3. The author of the essay discussed a short story called Enigma.
4. At the library, we learned that Enigma is part of a longer collection called Twenty Tales of Mystery.
5. Some of the stories in the book remind me of Edgar Allan Poe's poem The Raven.

Check Grammar, Spelling, and Mechanics

Proofread the passage. Check the spelling, the use of past tense verbs, and the punctuation of titles. Correct the mistakes.

Editing and Proofreading Marks

∧	Insert something.
∧ with comma	Add a comma.
∧ with semicolon	Add a semicolon.
⊙	Add a period.
⊙ with colon	Add a colon.
∨ with quotation marks	Add quotation marks.
∨ with apostrophe	Add an apostrophe.
≡	Capitalize.
/	Make lowercase.
delete mark	Delete.
¶	Make new paragraph.
oval	Check spelling.
replace mark	Replace with this.
∽	Change order.
#	Insert space.
close-up mark	Close up.

Once I decideed to write an article about code talkers, I began doing research. At the library, I writed down the titles of the books and articles I finded. My favorite book was called Wind Whisperers. I also seed a poem called Navajo Heroes.

At last, I was ready to write my article. I titleed it The War's Greatest Code. I was so excited to get to work that I typped five pages without stoping! Writeing an article is much easier than I thinked it would be.

Edit and Proofread Your Literary Response

Now edit and proofread your work.

Remember to Check

- ☐ past tense verbs
- ☐ spelling of verbs with *-ed* and *-ing* endings
- ☐ titles of literary works
- ☐ ______________________
- ☐ ______________________

1. Use a checklist as you edit and proofread. Add things you are working on to the checklist.

2. Look to see which errors are marked most often. Jot down your top three trouble spots.

____

____

____

3. Ask your teacher about ways to fix these mistakes, or check out the Grammar Handbook for information.

Focus on Spelling

Improve your spelling by following these steps.

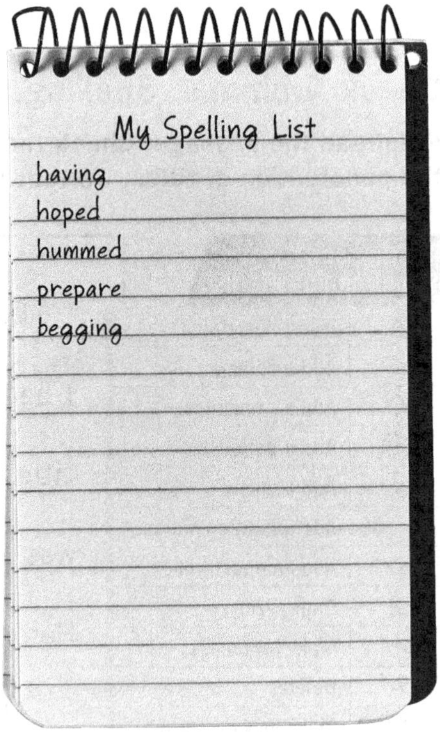

1. Create a personal spelling list. Record words that you misspelled. Look up the correct spelling in the dictionary and add these words to **My Spelling List**.

2. Pick twelve words. Write six sentences, using two of the words in each sentence. Wacky sentences are just fine! Double-check the spelling of the words. Then write six different sentences, using different pairs of spelling words.

3. Organize your words into different lists. List your words in alphabetical order. Next list them by the number of letters, from shortest word to longest. Spell the words aloud as you write them.

4. Make a personal word wall with your spelling words. List your words on chart paper. Read the words on your word wall. Then spell them letter by letter. Next close your eyes and spell them again, letter by letter. Open your eyes. Did you spell the word correctly?

5. Invent a story to help you remember difficult words. For example:

   Word cemetery

   Story got scared walking through the cemetery and yelled, "e-e-e!" as I ran away. (The word *cemetery* has three e's.)

Name ______________________________ Date ______________

Publish, Share, and Reflect

Publish and Share Your Literary Response

Check the final formats you used to publish your literary response. Then answer the following questions.

Publishing

What was the final format of your project?	How did you share your project?
☐ Wrote it neatly by hand	☐ Shared it with a large group
☐ Typed it on a computer	☐ Shared it with a small group

1. Whether you published it by hand or on the computer, what did you do to dress up your final project?

____

____

____

____

____

2. How did you share your work? What did you learn through sharing your work?

____

____

____

____

____

____

____

____

____

____

____

____

____

____

Reflect on Your Literary Response

Read your literary response. Then answer questions 1–6.

1. What do you like best about your work? ______

2. What did you do well? ______

3. What could you improve about your work? ______

4. Did you learn more about why this book means a lot to you? ______

5. Did you express your feelings well in your response? ______

6. Will you add your literary response to your Writing Portfolio? Explain your decision.

☐ Yes, I will add this to my Writing Portfolio.

☐ No, I will not add this to my Writing Portfolio.

Name ______________________ Date ______________

Analyze a Summary Paragraph

Read the article and each summary paragraph. Then answer the questions.

Rescue Cat?

by Lionel Caldwell

In December 2005, a police officer received a 9-1-1 call from Gary Rosheisen. But the officer did not hear anyone on the other end of the line. After redialing the number and still getting no response, he went to Gary's home.

When the officer arrived, Gary's orange cat was sitting next to the phone. Gary had fallen and couldn't get up.

The two men think the cat dialed 9-1-1. Apparently, Gary had tried many times to train the cat to press 9-1-1 on speed-dial. Luckily, the cat decided to show off its talent when its owner really needed help!

Feature Checklist

A good summary paragraph

- ☐ states the original writer's ideas in your own words
- ☐ includes all of the main ideas and important details
- ☐ leaves out details that are not important.

Summary Paragraphs

A. A police officer answered a 9-1-1 call. He arrived at the house and found a man on the floor, unable to move. The man said he had not called for help, so the two men concluded that the house cat had made the call. The owner had taught the cat to use the phone, and his efforts paid off in a big way.

B. A cat rescued his owner by calling 9-1-1. The owner was unable to move. Luckily, the cat decided to show off its talent.

1. Which summary paragraph is a good model?

____

____

____

____

____

2. What can you say about the wording in the two summary paragraphs? Is it always original?

____

____

____

____

____

____

____

3. Do the summaries include details that are not important?

____

____

____

____

____

____

____

Plan a Summary Paragraph

Use this page to plan a summary of a section of the article "Dogs at Work."

1. Choose a section of "Dogs at Work" to summarize. Then, take notes to keep track of the important ideas.

Title: ______________________________

Headings: ______________________________

Main Ideas: ______________________________

2. As you read, ask yourself questions. Write down the answers.

What is this section about? ______________________________

What's the point of this section? ______________________________

How could I say this part in just one sentence? ______________________________

3. Now, write key details from the article that you want to include in your summary.

Detail #1	Detail #2	Detail #3

Name ____________________ Date ____________

Draft a Summary Paragraph

Use your plan from page 150 to write the first draft of your summary paragraph for a section from "Dogs at Work."

Drafting Checklist

- ☐ State the original writer's ideas in your own words.
- ☐ Include all of the main ideas and important details.
- ☐ Leave out details that are not important.

Revise a Summary Paragraph

1. Use the checklist to evaluate this draft of a summary paragraph. What changes are needed?

____

____

____

____

____

Revising Checklist

- ☐ Are all the ideas important?
- ☐ Are the sentences concise and to the point?
- ☐ Can any ideas be combined?
- ☐ Are there any unnecessary details that need to be removed?

2. Revise the draft. Use revising marks to show your changes.

Revising

MARK	WHAT IT MEANS
∧	Insert something.
	Move to here.
	Replace with this.
	Take out.
¶	Make a new paragraph.

Positive Paws

Just being around a dog can be a positive experience for many people. The PAWSitive Therapy Troupe is welcomed in healthcare facilities because they provide positive experiences for patients. Therapy dogs help lift the spirits of people who are sick. People who are not sick can enjoy the dogs too. Patients benefit from interacting with the dogs. Studies have shown that being active with animals can promote relaxation. It can also reduce anxiety and distract people from pain. In general the dogs provide unconditional love and acceptance.

3. Now use the checklist to help you revise the draft of your summary paragraph on page 151.

Name ______________________________ Date ______________

Edit and Proofread

Grammar Workout: Check Object Pronouns

Complete each pair of sentences with an object pronoun. Circle the noun or noun phrase from the first sentence that the object pronoun refers to.

OBJECT PRONOUNS	
me	us
you	you
him, her, it	them

1. *The Wizard of Oz* is a great book. I read __________ last summer and then I saw the movie.

2. Dorothy and Toto were inseparable. Toto would follow __________ wherever she went.

3. Terry was a female actor dog. People trained __________ to perform tricks.

4. Actor dogs require a lot of training. Trainers give __________ treats as a reward.

Spelling Workout: Check Words Ending in *-y*

Complete the article. Add the correct form of the noun or verb in parentheses.

In 1939, Terry ____________ **(play)** Toto in *The Wizard of Oz*. There are many actor dogs today. An owner of an actor dog ____________ **(carry)** a bag filled with ____________ **(accessory)** to groom the animal. Often, these dogs belong to ____________ **(agency)** that find work for them. With all this work and preparation, I wonder if these dogs are really ____________ **(enjoy)** themselves!

Mechanics Workout: Check Apostrophes with Contractions

Write contractions for the words in parentheses.

1. Terry was an actor dog. ____________ famous for playing Toto in *The Wizard of Oz*. **(She is)**

2. She ____________ star only in that movie. **(did not)**

3. We learned about actor dogs. ____________ very disciplined. **(They are)**

4. I tried to train my dog. He ____________ give me his paw to save his life! **(could not)**

5. I ____________ want my dog to be a film star. **(would not)** ____________ never let that happen. **(I will)**

Check Grammar, Spelling, and Mechanics

Proofread the passage. Check the use of object pronouns, the spelling of words ending in *-y*, and the use of apostrophes with contractions. Correct the mistakes.

Editing and Proofreading Marks

^	Insert something.
^,	Add a comma.
^;	Add a semicolon.
⊙	Add a period.
(:)	Add a colon.
“ ”	Add quotation marks.
’	Add an apostrophe.
≡	Capitalize.
/	Make lowercase.
℘	Delete.
¶	Make new paragraph.
◯	Check spelling.
^‾	Replace with this.
∿	Change order.
#	Insert space.
⁐	Close up.

I'am reading one of the weirdest autobiographyes ever written. Its "written" by Terry, the dog who plaied Toto in *The Wizard of Oz*. The movie was very successful and people loved she. She was paid a lot. Just think that many actors' salaryes were half of Terry's! I could nt believe the storyes about her. She didnt like the wind machines used on set, so she avoided their all the time. Even though Terry became a famous star, she wasnt very outgoing. Actually, she was very shy! Her owner had to pull she from under the bed to train him.

Name ______________________________ Date ______________

Edit and Proofread Your Summary Paragraph

Now edit and proofread your work.

Remember to Check

- ☐ object pronouns
- ☐ words ending in *-y*
- ☐ apostrophes with contractions
- ☐ ______________________
- ☐ ______________________

1. Use a checklist as you edit and proofread. Add things you are working on to the checklist.
2. Look to see which errors are marked most often. Jot down your top three trouble spots.

____

____

____

3. Ask your teacher about ways to fix these mistakes, or check out the Grammar Handbook for information.

Focus on Spelling

Improve your spelling by following these steps.

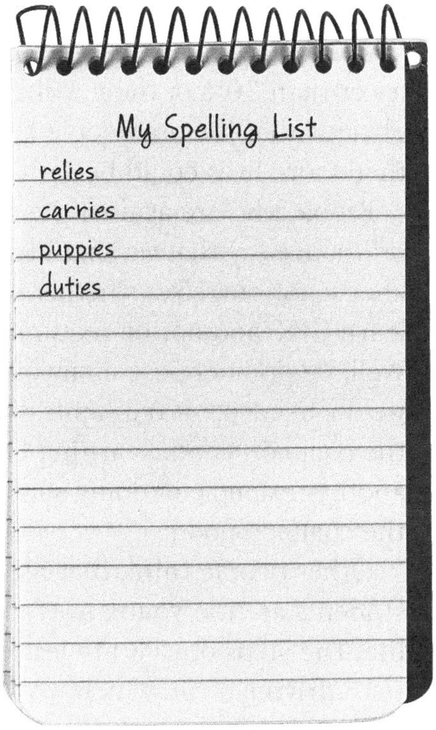

1. Create a personal spelling list. Record words that you misspelled. Look up correct spelling in the dictionary and add these words to **My Spelling List**.
2. Pick twelve words. Write each word four times. First write it in all lowercase letters. Next write it in all capital letters. After that, write the vowels in lowercase and consonants in uppercase. Last, write the word using fancy letters that you create on your own. For example, your letters can be curly or tall and skinny.
3. Work with a partner to play **I'm Thinking of a Spelling Word**. Take turns giving each other clues. Some clues might be *I'm thinking of a word that rhymes with . . .*, or *I'm thinking of a word that means . . .* With each clue, the answer should include the word and its spelling.
4. Work with a partner to play a scrambled letter game. Take each other's spelling words and write them in scrambled form. See which one of you can unscramble all the words first.
5. Use an audio recorder and record your words and their spelling. Then listen to your tape, checking to see that you spell each word correctly.

Analyze a Letter to the Editor

What makes this letter to the editor a good model? Read the letter to the editor and answer the questions.

Aug. 6, 2014

To the Editor,

The city council should pass the CPR ordinance, which will require high school seniors to pass a CPR test before they graduate. This requirement is important because CPR (cardio-pulmonary resuscitation) can help a person whose heart may have stopped beating to stay alive.

According to the American Heart Association, over 1.5 million heart attacks and 7 million injuries that may require CPR happen each year. Almost 70% of these emergencies happen at home when a family member might help. Sadly, 94% of people who have a heart attack outside of a hospital die before reaching one, and fewer than 30% of them will get CPR. It's obvious that if more people knew CPR, then more lives could be saved.

People who are against the CPR ordinance say that we should be able to choose for ourselves whether we want to learn CPR, and not be required to learn it. Well, we don't choose many of the things we do, like stop at red lights. We do it for the common good. Learning CPR is just another example of doing something for the common good.

Other people think that high school students are too young to try to save a life. The steps of CPR are less complicated than driving a car, which we trust to students even younger than seniors. Also, people suffering a heart attack cannot be put in greater danger than they are already in.

I encourage the city council to pass this ordinance for the common good and the good health of our community.

Sincerely,
Penelope Baker

Feature Checklist

A good letter to the editor

- ❑ clearly states an opinion about a subject
- ❑ includes reasons and evidence to support the opinion
- ❑ uses a formal style and the proper format
- ❑ includes a closing statement that restates and supports the opinion

1. Does this letter follow the proper letter-to-the-editor format? Explain.

____

____

____

____

2. How would you describe the style of this letter? What makes you think so?

____

____

____

____

____

3. What does the writer share about her thoughts?

____

____

____

____

____

____

____

Name ________________________________ Date ____________

Plan a Letter to the Editor

Use pages 157–158 to plan your letter to the editor.

1. For a focused letter to the editor, choose one issue that you have a strong opinion about. Think about things you know, read, or hear about, and write them below. Circle the idea you want to write about.

Ideas:

____

____

____

____

____

2. Use the T Chart below to list reasons for your opinion and evidence to support it.

T Chart

Opinion:	
Reasons for Opinion	Evidence to Support Opinion

3. Use the T Chart below to list opposing views other people might have to your opinion. How would you respond to each of the opposing views? Think about what you might say and expand the T Chart to include each logical response.

T Chart

Opinion:	
Opposing Views:	Logical Response:

Name ________________ Date ________

Draft a Letter to the Editor

Use your plan from pages 157–158 to write the first draft of your letter to the editor.

Drafting Checklist

- ☐ Clearly states an opinion about a subject.
- ☐ Includes reasons and evidence to support the opinion.
- ☐ Uses a formal style and the proper format.
- ☐ Includes a closing statement that restates the opinion.

Revise a Letter to the Editor

1. Use the checklist to evaluate this draft of a letter to the editor. What changes are needed?

____

____

____

____

____

Revising Checklist

- ❑ Is the tone too casual and informal?
- ❑ Is the opinion clear?
- ❑ Do reasons and evidence need to be added to support the opinion?
- ❑ Should any confusing or unclear information be removed?

2. Revise the draft. Use revising marks to show your changes.

Revising

MARK	WHAT IT MEANS
^	Insert something.
	Move to here.
	Replace with this.
	Take out.
¶	Make a new paragraph.

October 8, 2014

Dear Editor,

I am writing about your newspaper's "Person-of-the-Year" award. I am writing to nominate Anna Westlake. She is awesome! Our local Coast Guard captain has rescued over ten people from accidents just this year. The water is dangerous.

Some people will say that Westlake is "just doing her job," but her job is very important and she does it really well. She also does it with a smile. I think those reasons make her deserving of this award.

Sincerely,

Gabriella Torres

3. Now use the checklist to help you revise the draft of your letter to the editor on page 159.

Name ______________________________ Date ______________

Edit and Proofread

Grammar Workout: Check Prepositional Phrases

Write a prepositional phrase to complete each sentence.

SOME PREPOSITIONS		
about	for	near
around	in	to
at	on	with

If you want to organize a food drive ______________, you can. Contact your teacher ______________. Then, you can look online to find volunteer organizations ______________. They can tell you everything you need to know______________. You can present your idea ______________ and get started helping your community!

Spelling Workout: Check Sound-Alike Words

Complete each sentence about volunteer work. Use the correct word.

1. ____________ help at the food drive will be very much appreciated.
   You're/Your

2. In a food drive, every small contribution ____________ up.
   adds/ads

3. Members of the ____________ discussed how to organize the food drive at school.
   board/bored

4. I ____________ at this year's result and I found out we raised more than last year!
   peaked/peeked

5. I talked with the school ____________ , and she is willing to help with the food drive.
   principal/principle

Mechanics Workout: Check Use of Commas and Dashes

Edit this letter. Add a comma or a dash where necessary.

April 3, 2008

Dear Editor

I want to thank the Daily Record for helping to make our school's food drive a great success your stories about the drive brought in many contributions. My classmates and I have been busy collecting all sorts of food items canned food, rice, beans, etc. Thank you again for your help. Call me, OK?

Yours truly

Laura Benson

Check Grammar, Spelling, and Mechanics

Proofread the passage. Add prepositional phrases and check for sound-alike words, commas, and dashes. Correct the mistakes.

Editing and Proofreading Marks

^	Insert something.
^ (comma)	Add a comma.
^ (semicolon)	Add a semicolon.
⊙	Add a period.
(:)	Add a colon.
∜ ∜	Add quotation marks.
∜	Add an apostrophe.
≡	Capitalize.
/	Make lowercase.
℘	Delete.
¶	Make new paragraph.
⬭	Check spelling.
⌃‾	Replace with this.
∽	Change order.
#	Insert space.
⁐	Close up.

Dear Vicki

It's great that you like your knew school! I've been busy too. I'm working for a worthy cause a food drive. Thankfully, the school aloud us to use the gym for donations. We were able to rays a lot of money and collect tons of food. The second phase starts tomorrow, though. I will be ceiling boxes!

I hope to hear from you soon.

Your friend

Jonah

Name ______________________________ Date ______________

Edit and Proofread Your Letter to the Editor

Now edit and proofread your work.

Remember to Check

❑ prepositional phrases
❑ sound-alike words
❑ use of commas and dashes
❑ ______________________
❑ ______________________

1. Use a checklist as you edit and proofread. Add things you are working on to the checklist.

2. Look to see which errors are marked most often. Jot down your top three trouble spots.

____

____

____

3. Ask your teacher about ways to fix these mistakes, or check out the Grammar Handbook for information.

Focus on Spelling

Improve your spelling by following these steps.

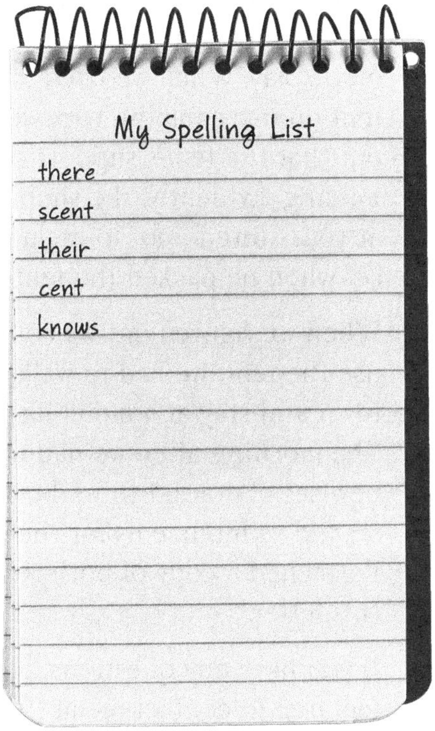

1. Create a personal spelling list. Record words that you misspelled. Look up correct spelling in the dictionary and add these words to **My Spelling List**.

2. Pick twelve words. Make a colorful display of the words. Get a sheet of chart paper. Write each word three times in a different color.

3. Work with a partner to play **Spelling Tic-Tac-Toe**. Draw a tic-tac-toe board. Take turns asking each other to spell words. When a player spells a word correctly, that player gets to mark an X or an O on the game board.

4. Write the letters for each word on separate squares of paper. Attach the letters for each word to each other with a paper clip. Unscramble the letters to spell each of your words.

5. Invent your own memory strategy for difficult words. Think of a good way to remember *why* letters appear or do not appear in a word. For example:

Word	**Explanation**
dessert	"It has two s's for <u>s</u>weet <u>s</u>tuff!"

Analyze a Business Letter

What makes this business letter a good model? Read the business letter and answer the questions.

204 Channing St.
Sewanee, TN 37375
August 6, 2014

Lidia Margoulis, Customer Service
Best Gear, Inc.
1200 Washington Blvd.
Knoxville, TN 37901

Dear Ms. Margoulis:

On July 25, 2014, my family and I purchased a tent from your store. We were planning a camping trip, so we bought your Zodiac Tent Model 12. The tent was on sale because it was on display. When we tried to pitch the tent on our camping trip, we found out that the tent's support poles were missing. Evidently, the shop assistant at your store forgot to include the pole set when he packed the tent for us.

When we figured out we could not use the tent, we had to walk back to town and stay at a motel for the night. The morning after, we had to buy a new set of poles. I think Best Gear should reimburse us for the expenses. I attached a copy of both receipts to this letter.

If you have any questions, please feel free to contact me at (931) 555-6447. My family has frequented your store for years, and I am sure you will understand the situation. I look forward to hearing from you.

Sincerely,
Albert Barbaro
Albert Barbaro

Feature Checklist

A good business letter

- ❑ makes a claim and states the situation clearly
- ❑ provides evidence that develops and supports the writer's claim
- ❑ uses formal language and a polite tone
- ❑ follows the standard business-letter format.

1. Does the writer make a claim and state the situation clearly? Explain.

____
____
____
____
____
____

2. What reasons does the writer give for wanting a refund for his family's expenses?

____
____
____
____
____
____
____

3. How does this model follow the form of a standard business letter?

____
____
____
____
____
____
____

Name ______________________________ Date ______________

Plan a Business Letter

Use this page to plan your business letter.

1. Plan what you'll say about the problem. Answer each question in this list.

Question	**Answer**
What did I buy?	______________________
When did I buy it?	______________________
Where did I buy it?	______________________
What was the problem?	______________________
Why was it a problem?	______________________

2. Use the phone, Internet, or other resources to find out whom to contact about the problem. Write down that person's name, address, and any other important contact information.

Name of contact: ______________________________

Address: ______________________________

____

Other information: ______________________________

____

3. Make a list of possible solutions to your problem. Then, decide on the solution you want. Circle the solution you choose.

Possible Solutions

1. ______________________________

____

2. ______________________________

____

3. ______________________________

____

Draft a Business Letter

Use your plan from page 165 to write the first draft of your business letter.

Drafting Checklist

- ❑ Include your address.
- ❑ Include the name and address of the person you are writing to.
- ❑ Use a formal greeting.
- ❑ State the problem or situation clearly. Give reasons for the possible solutions you suggest.
- ❑ Use a formal and polite tone.
- ❑ Use a formal closing. Sign and type your name.

:

Name ______________________ Date ______________

Revise a Business Letter

1. Use the checklist to evaluate this draft of a business letter. What changes are needed?

____

____

____

____

____

Revising Checklist

- ❑ Is the tone polite and formal?
- ❑ Are the problem and desired solution clear?
- ❑ Is there any unnecessary information that should be taken out?
- ❑ Should any ideas be consolidated to make the letter more concise?

2. Revise the draft. Use revising marks to show your changes.

Revising

MARK	WHAT IT MEANS
∧	Insert something.
(arrow with loop)	Move to here.
(caret with line)	Replace with this.
(line with loop)	Take out.
¶	Make a new paragraph.

I am writing about a problem with a jacket that I bought from U Sport in Placerville, Connecticut. I bought it on October 17 in preparation for the winter. The jacket is supposed to be weather-proof. I wore it during a light rain. I was outside for only ten minutes, but I was soaked!

The jacket's material is now permanently damaged and stained because of the rain. It doesn't even keep me warm anymore. I am enclosing the damaged jacket. I am also sending a copy of the receipt. Please send me a refund, but don't send me a new jacket. Thank you for your attention to this problem.

3. Now use the checklist to help you revise the draft of your business letter on page 166.

Edit and Proofread

Grammar Workout: Check Subject and Object Pronouns

Complete each pair of sentences with a pronoun. Circle the noun or noun phrase from the first sentence that the pronoun refers to.

1. The flashlight failed. I tried to turn ____________ on, but I couldn't.

2. My family and I were afraid to get lost. ____________ proceeded very carefully.

3. We had some expenses. I hope the store reimburses us for all of ____________ .

4. Hikers need to be well equipped. ____________ must be prepared if danger arises.

Spelling Workout: Check Words with Greek or Latin Roots

Find the spelling error in each sentence. Write the misspelled word correctly.

LATIN ROOT	MEANING
scrib, script	write
ques	ask, seek
GREEK ROOT	**MEANING**
chrono	time
logo	word, reason, study

1. I skribbled a few notes before writing the letter. ____________

2. I have a qustion about reimbursement policies. ____________

3. In my letter, I detailed the cronology of the facts. ____________

4. I hope they won't think my reasons for complaining are illougical. ____________

Edit and Proofread, continued

Mechanics Workout: Check Colons and Semicolons

Edit this letter. Add colons and semicolons where necessary.

Dear Mr. Kitano

I wrote you two weeks ago about reimbursing me for a faulty flashlight so far you have not responded. Enclosed are the following the receipt for the flashlight a picture of it, showing the broken piece and a copy of the guarantee. If you need more information please call me at (301) 555-8894 after 430 P.M.

Sincerely,

Andreas Linden

Check Grammar, Spelling, and Mechanics

Proofread the passage. Check for subject and object pronouns, words with Greek or Latin roots, and colons and semicolons. Correct the mistakes.

Editing and Proofreading Marks

Mark	Meaning
^	Insert something.
^ with comma	Add a comma.
^ with semicolon	Add a semicolon.
⊙	Add a period.
(:)	Add a colon.
ˇ" ˇ"	Add quotation marks.
ˇ'	Add an apostrophe.
≡	Capitalize.
/	Make lowercase.
℘	Delete.
¶	Make new paragraph.
◯	Check spelling.
⌃‾	Replace with this.
∾	Change order.
#	Insert space.
⊂⊃	Close up.

Dear Mr. Goldman

Thank you for sending I a replacement flashlight. Unfortunately, the flashlight you sent is not the one us recuested. The model we purchased was more expensive than the one you sent we the other flashlight was also brighter than this one. Call I on my cell fone anytime to discuss this matter.

Edit and Proofread Your Business Letter

Now edit and proofread your work.

1. Use a checklist as you edit and proofread. Add things you are working on to the checklist.

2. Look to see which errors are marked most often. Jot down your top three trouble spots.

____

____

____

3. Ask your teacher about ways to fix these mistakes, or check out the Grammar Handbook for information.

Remember to Check

- ☐ subject and object pronouns
- ☐ words with Greek or Latin roots
- ☐ colons and semicolons
- ☐ ______________
- ☐ ______________

Focus on Spelling

Improve your spelling by following these steps.

1. Create a personal spelling list. Record words that you misspelled. Look up correct spelling in the dictionary and add these words to **My Spelling List**.

2. Pick twelve words. Make each word look interesting and special by tracing it five times. Write the word in one color. Then trace it four more times in four different colors. Say each letter to yourself as you trace it.

3. Work with a partner to play **Spelling Catch**. Pitch words to each other by saying "Here's the windup. Here's the pitch. The word is . . ." Take turns pitching. The first "batter" to spell ten words correctly wins.

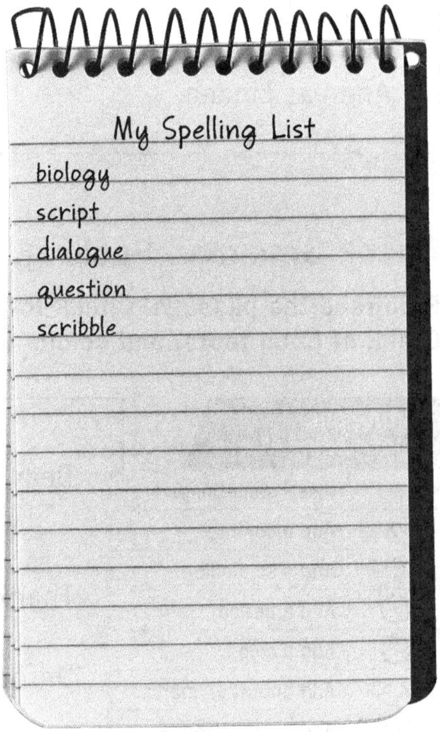

4. Write each spelling word three times. The first time just write the word. The second time, write it and then circle all the consonants. The third time, write it and circle all the vowels.

5. Play **Memory** to help you remember your words. Write each spelling word on two different index cards. Mix up the cards and place them face down. Turn the cards over two at a time. Your goal is to find the matching cards. Say and spell the words on the cards you turn over. If you make a match, remove those cards from the game. You've won when you've removed all the cards.

Name ______________________ Date ______________

Analyze Chronological-Order Paragraphs

What makes these paragraphs a good model? Read the paragraphs and answer the questions.

Make Way for the WNBA

by Lamont Wayne

In 1892, women's basketball became an official sport. Senda Berenson Abbott established women's rules and introduced the first regulated game at Smith College. Since then, women's basketball has gained popularity and is now a professional sport.

At first, most women's basketball games were held between college teams. The sport did not gain worldwide attention until 1976. That year, women's basketball debuted at the Montreal Olympics.

Two years later, the first professional basketball league for women was formed. The Women's Professional Basketball League (WBL) lasted only three seasons. Still, the WBL proved that there was a place for women in professional basketball.

In 1996, the National Basketball Association (NBA) approved the idea of the Women's National Basketball Association (WNBA). By aligning with the hugely popular NBA, the WNBA had a great chance for success. During the first season, eight WNBA teams were introduced.

Today, the WNBA has 12 teams. The league continues to gain popularity. Games are broadcasted to nearly 60 million fans in 167 countries. WNBA merchandise is sold in major retail stores. Maybe one day the women's league will be just as popular as the men's league.

Feature Checklist

Paragraphs in chronological order

- ❑ each have a main idea and supporting details
- ❑ describe events in the order in which they happened
- ❑ use sequence words and dates to show the order of events.

1. What are these paragraphs about?

____

____

____

____

2. The writer presents events in chronological order. What happened on each date?

1976: ______________________

____

____

1978: ______________________

____

____

1996: ______________________

____

____

Today: ______________________

____

____

3. In addition to dates, what signal words does the writer use to show order of events?

____

____

____

Plan Chronological-Order Paragraphs

Use pages 172–173 to plan your chronological-order paragraph.

1. Focus on one thing about the sport you have chosen, and avoid including information that is general knowledge. Use the diagram to help you narrow your topic.

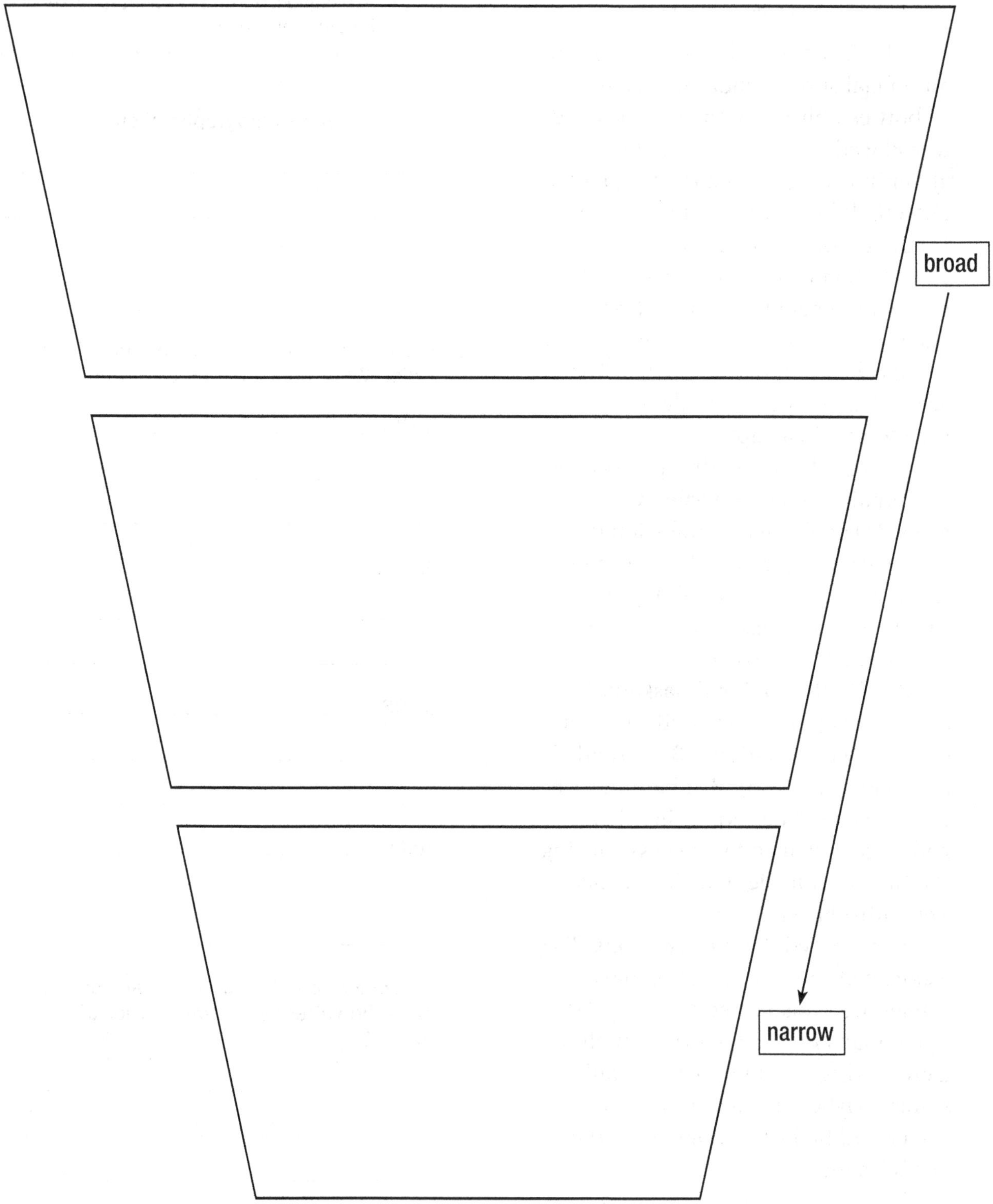

Name ______________________________ Date ______________

Plan Chronological-Order Paragraphs, continued

2. Now use a sequence chain or a time line to organize your facts in chronological order.

Sequence Chain **Time Line**

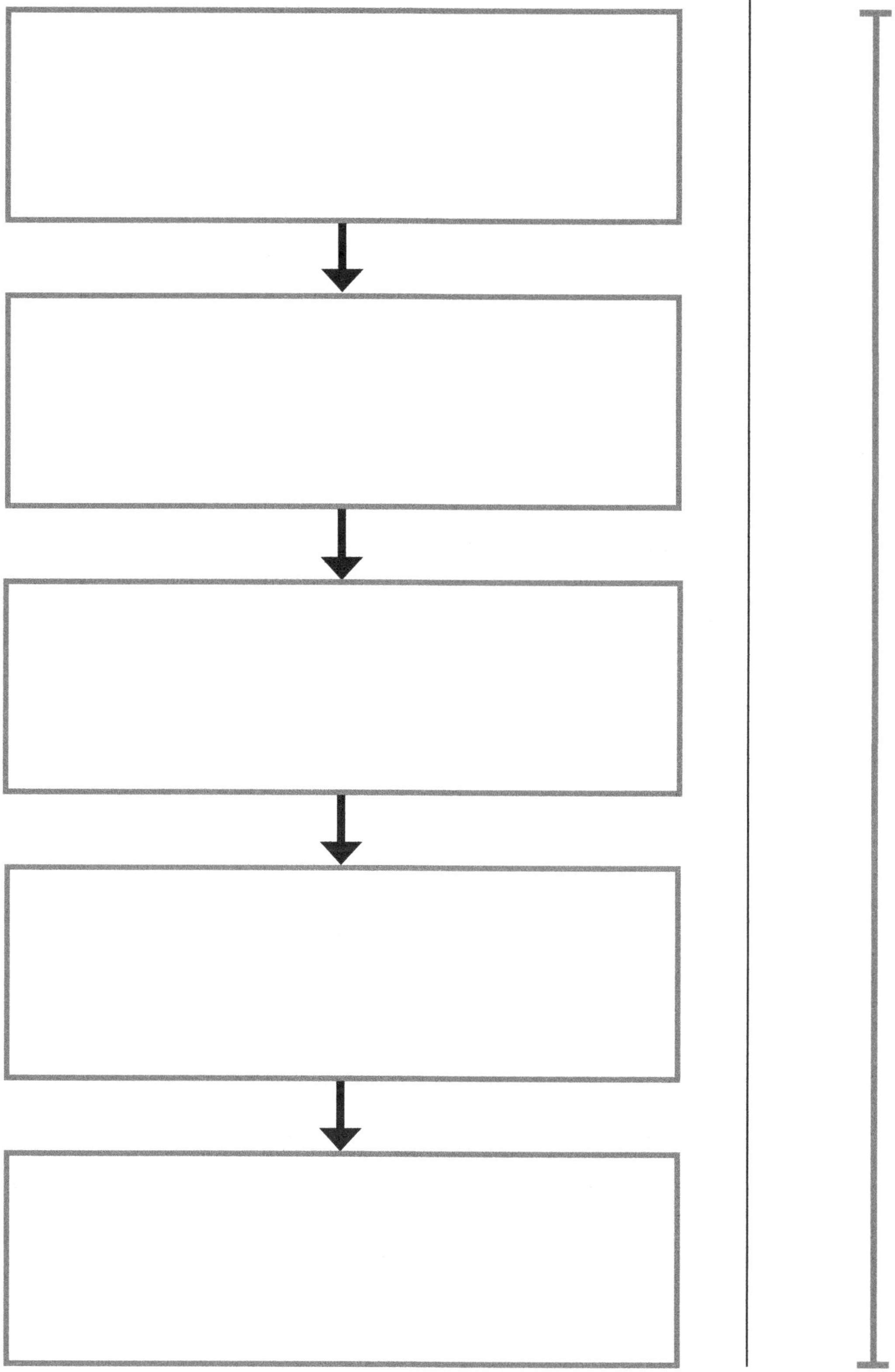

Draft Chronological-Order Paragraphs

Use your plan from pages 172–173 to write the first draft of your paragraphs in chronological order. Use additional sheets of paper if you need to.

Drafting Checklist

- ☐ Describe events in the order in which they happen.
- ☐ Use sequence words and dates to show the order of events.
- ☐ Add plenty of details to make your paragraphs interesting.

Name ______________________________ Date ______________

Revise Chronological-Order Paragraphs

1. Use the checklist to evaluate this draft of a paragraph in chronological order. What changes are needed?

____

____

____

____

____

Revising Checklist

- ☐ Did you describe events in the order in which they happened?
- ☐ Did you use sequence words and dates to show the order of events?
- ☐ Do you need to add more details to describe what happened?

2. Revise the draft. Use revising marks to show your changes.

Revising

MARK	WHAT IT MEANS
∧	Insert something.
↶⊂⊃	Move to here.
⌃⎯	Replace with this.
⎯ℓ	Take out.
¶	Make a new paragraph.

Tim Duncan

Tim Duncan is one of the best power forwards in the NBA. Born in the U.S. Virgin Islands, Duncan spent his early years training as a swimmer. In 1989, Hurricane Hugo destroyed the only pool near his home, so Duncan turned to basketball. He was drafted by the San Antonio Spurs in 1997 and has played there ever since. First, he received an offer to play on the team at at Wake Forest University in North Carolina. Duncan played there for four years and earned a degree in psychology before joining the NBA.

3. Now use the checklist to help you revise the draft of your chronological-order paragraphs on page 174.

Edit and Proofread

Grammar Workout: Check Verb Tenses

To complete each sentence, write the correct tense of the verb in parentheses.

1. I wanted to join the tennis team, so I ____________ (practice) a lot that first year.

2. I ____________ (serve) so many times that my arm hurt every day.

3. It paid off, though, because I made the team and ____________ (play) very well at the tournament.

4. Now, I don't need to practice so hard, so I ____________ (have) time to do other stuff.

5. After school, some days I just ____________ (hang) around with my friends and do nothing.

6. Tennis comes so naturally to me now, that next year maybe I ____________ (try) out for the hockey team.

Spelling Workout: Check Words You Have to Know or Look Up

Circle the correct spelling of each word. Use a dictionary if you need to.

1. comman	common	commen
2. leval	levil	level
3. cactos	cactis	cactus
4. actress	actriss	actruss
5. bacan	bacun	bacon
6. humin	human	humon
7. teller	tellar	tellor
8. funnel	funnal	funnul

Name ______________________________ Date ______________

Edit and Proofread, continued

Mechanics Workout: Check for Commas Before Conjunctions

Add the missing comma to each sentence.

1. The first practice is after school and I'm so excited.

2. This is what I've looked forward to all year but I have to admit I'm a little nervous.

3. Will I impress the rest of the team or will I make a fool of myself?

4. There's a lot to worry about but I'll forget to worry once I start playing.

5. My teammates and I will practice and we'll improve our skills.

6. We'll have to remember to work hard or Coach will remind us!

Check Grammar, Spelling, and Mechanics

Proofread the passage. Check the spelling, the use of verb tenses, and the use of commas before conjunctions. Correct the mistakes.

Editing and Proofreading Marks

∧	Insert something.
∧ with comma	Add a comma.
∧ with semicolon	Add a semicolon.
⊙	Add a period.
⊙ with colon	Add a colon.
∨ ∨ with quotation marks	Add quotation marks.
∨ with apostrophe	Add an apostrophe.
≡	Capitalize.
/	Make lowercase.
℘	Delete.
¶	Make new paragraph.
◯	Spell out.
replace mark	Replace with this.
∽	Change order.
#	Insert space.
⁀‿	Close up.

The weather was awfel during our first practice but we work hard anyway. First, we stretched from head to foot. We run uround the track several times and I got really tired. Our final activity was on the tennus court. Coach Harris watched each of us swing a racket and gives us advice on how to hold it. I can already tell that my swing is improving but it take a long time before I am able to hit the ball every time. I guess that's why practice is so important.

Edit and Proofread Your Chronological-Order Paragraphs

Now edit and proofread your work.

1. Use a checklist as you edit and proofread. Add things you are working on to the checklist.

2. Look to see which errors are marked most often. Jot down your top three trouble spots.

____

____

____

3. Ask your teacher about ways to fix these mistakes, or check out the Grammar Handbook for information.

Remember to Check

- ☐ verb tenses
- ☐ spelling of words you have to know or look up
- ☐ commas before conjunctions
- ☐ ____________________
- ☐ ____________________

Focus on Spelling

Improve your spelling by following these steps.

1. Create a personal spelling list. Record words that you misspelled. Look up correct spelling in the dictionary and add these words to **My Spelling List**.

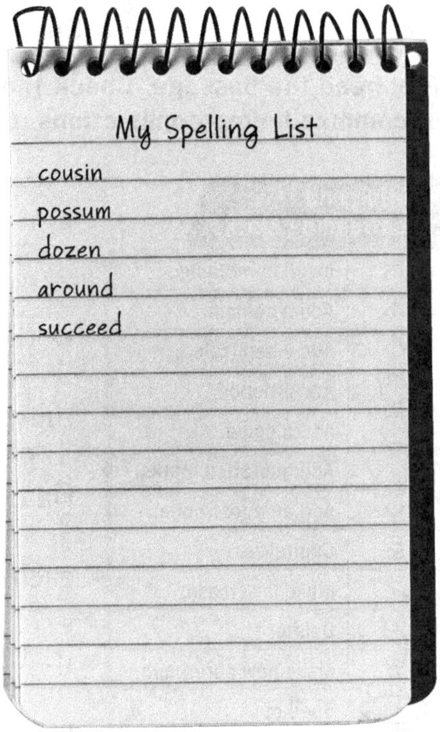

2. Pick twelve words. Focus on four words each day. Write your words before each meal and check the spelling. At the end of the week, try writing all twelve words.

3. Work with a partner to play **Spelling Behind Your Back**. Have a partner stand with his or her back to the board. List spelling words on the board. Say each word and ask your partner to spell it. Switch roles.

4. Organize your words into lists. List them from shortest to longest word. Next, list them from easiest to hardest. Then list them in reverse alphabetical order.

5. Invent your own acronyms. Think of a word that begins with each letter. The words in the correct order should be easy for you to remember. For example:

Spelling word	Acronym
ocean	octopus, coral, eel are near

Name ______________________ Date ______________

Analyze a Biography

What makes this biography a good model? Read the biography and answer the questions.

My Grandfather: Jorge Cortez

by Paul Ruiz

Jorge Cortez was born in Havana, Cuba, in 1941. He and his family moved to New York City two years later. At an early age, Jorge showed an extreme interest in sports. He especially loved baseball. Jorge was not very good at playing baseball, but he knew everything about the game. He often impressed his friends by reciting the names, numbers, and batting averages of the entire New York Yankees' roster.

When Jorge got to high school, his English teacher, Mrs. Hanes, noticed that Jorge had other talents. In addition to knowing a lot about baseball, Jorge was also a very good writer. Mrs. Hanes was impressed with how well Jorge explained details and expressed his ideas. She suggested he combine his passion for baseball with his talent for writing.

Jorge took Mrs. Hanes's advice. He started writing a sports column for his school newspaper. His column covered the school's sports teams as well as some local baseball teams. Jorge's column was so well liked that the *Star Reporter,* a local newspaper, ran one of his articles in their August 25, 1957 issue.

Feature Checklist

A good biography

- ❑ gives background information about the person
- ❑ tells about important events in the person's life
- ❑ presents events in chronological order.

1. **What type of background information about the person does the writer give?**

____

____

____

____

____

2. **How can you tell that this biography is well researched?**

____

____

____

____

____

3. **How does the writer make the order of events clear?**

____

____

____

____

____

After he graduated from high school, Jorge enrolled at New York University. He majored in journalism. While in school, Jorge learned to write about more than just baseball. He was taught how to report on local and national events as well as other types of news.

Jorge graduated from college in 1963. He and two former classmates started their own newspaper called the *Cuban Beat*. The paper focused on Cuban-American matters. Jorge and his friends produced 167 issues of the *Cuban Beat* before moving on to other projects.

In 1972, Jorge returned to his roots. He began writing a weekly sports column for the *Star Reporter*, the same newspaper that had printed his very first article. Jorge's column ran for 30 years. It was considered a favorite among the newspaper's readers.

Jorge retired from journalism in 2002. Now he enjoys spending more time with his family. Although he doesn't write about baseball anymore, Jorge still loves to watch it.

4. Are all of the events from Jorge Cortez's life presented in chronological order? Explain your answer.

____

____

____

____

5. Finish filling out the events from Jorge Cortez's life.

1941: born in Cuba

____

1957: ______________________________

____

1963: ______________________________

____

1972: ______________________________

____

2002: ______________________________

____

Name ______________________ Date ____________

Evaluate for Voice and Style

Read the biography below. Use the rubric on page 182 to score the biography for voice and style. Then answer the questions.

Score	1	2	3	4

The Say Hey Kid

Willie Mays is considered by many to be one of the greatest baseball players ever. Nicknamed the "Say Hey Kid," Mays learned how to catch before he could walk. Mays signed with the New York Giants. And, oh yeah, he also graduated from high school on that day!

It took Mays a while to adjust to playing in the Major Leagues. He didn't get a single hit his first 12 times at bat. But his 13th time, he hit a home run over the left-field fence. By the end of his first year, he had hit another 19 balls out of the park. His fielding was also becoming legendary. In a game against Pittsburgh, he caught a 475-foot hit with his bare hand. That year Mays was voted the National League's Rookie of the Year.

Mays went on to have a spectacular and long-lasting baseball career. He could do the five things necessary to become a baseball legend. He could hit, hit with power, run, catch, and throw. He was a 20-time All Star and a 12-time Gold Glove winner. Mays was inducted into the Baseball Hall of Fame in 1979. He got in the first year he was eligible. Awesome!

1. Explain the reasons for your score.

____

2. Which verbs in the second paragraph would you change to make the writing more powerful?

____

3. Look at the sentences in the third paragraph. Are they varied enough? Do they flow well together? What changes would you make?

____

Writing Rubric

Voice and Style		
	Does the writing have a clear voice and is it the best style for the type of writing?	Is the language interesting and are the words and sentences appropriate for the purpose, audience, and type of writing?
4 Wow!	The writing fully engages the reader with its individual voice. The writing style is best for the type of writing.	**The words and sentences are interesting and appropriate to the purpose and audience.** • The words are precise and engaging. • The sentences are varied and flow together smoothly.
3 Ahh.	Most of the writing engages the reader with an individual voice. The writing style is mostly best for the type of writing.	**Most of the words and sentences are interesting and appropriate to the purpose and audience.** • Most words are precise and engaging. • Most sentences are varied and flow together.
2 Hmm.	Some of the writing engages the reader, but it has no individual voice and the style is not best for the writing type.	**Some of the words and sentences are interesting and appropriate to the purpose and audience.** • Some words are precise and engaging. • Some sentences are varied, but the flow could be smoother.
1 Huh?	The writing does not engage the reader.	**Few or none of the words and sentences are appropriate to the purpose and audience.** • The words are often vague and dull. • The sentences lack variety and do not flow together.

Name ______________________ Date ____________

Raise the Score

1. Use the rubric on page 182 to evaluate and score this biography.

Score	1	2	3	4

Baseball Secret Agent

Morris "Moe" Berg is an interesting baseball player. He was like straight out of a movie or something.

Born in 1902, Berg was good at languages. He spoke more than nine languages, including French, Italian, Spanish, Portuguese, German, Japanese, Latin, Greek, and Sanskrit.

After graduating college, Berg played baseball for the Brooklyn Robins. He played for 16 years for various teams. He also earned his law degree.

At 39, Berg went to work for the government. He was an Ambassador of Goodwill to Latin America. He also worked for the Office of Strategic Service (OSS). Today, the OSS is called the Central Intelligence Agency, or CIA.

During World War II, he went to a talk by Werner Heisenberg. Heisenberg was a German physicist. Berg was going to shoot Heisenberg if he felt the Germans were close to developing a nuclear weapon. But, don't worry, he didn't.

When the war ended, Berg quit the OSS and never worked again. He even declined the Medal of Merit when it was offered to him. He certainly was unique.

2. Explain what the writer should do to raise the score:

____

____

____

____

____

____

3. **Now revise the biography on page 183 to improve its voice and style. Write your revised biography here.**

Name ______________________ Date ____________

Choose the Right Voice

A. Study the FATP chart below. Then read the editorial at right and answer the questions.

FATP Chart

Form: editorial

Audience: readers of school newspaper

Topic: Shoeless Joe Jackson

Purpose: to persuade

1. Is the writer's tone appropriate for the audience? Explain your answer.

____

____

____

____

____

____

____

____

2. Does the word choice seem appropriate for a persuasive piece? Explain your answer.

____

____

____

____

____

____

____

____

____

3. If you answered yes to Item 2, circle examples of appropriate voice in the text. If you answered no, use revising marks to show how you would change it.

"Shoeless Joe" Innocent!

In 1919, the Chicago White Sox unexpectedly lost the World Series to the Cincinnati Reds. "Shoeless Joe" Jackson and seven other teammates were accused of throwing the games, or losing them on purpose, and were banned from baseball for life.

Looking at the facts, I'm sure you will agree with me that Jackson's performance in that series shows that he could not possibly have been involved with this scandal.

In 1919, Jackson hit a .351 average. In the World Series, he hit .375 and didn't make one single error fielding! Surely a player who was trying to lose would make at least one error. He also hit the only home run of the series. How is that "throwing the game"?

Jackson was acquitted of any charges by a Chicago grand jury. But Commissioner Landis ignored the ruling. He banned Jackson from baseball for life. This makes Jackson ineligible for the Hall of Fame.

Jackson holds the record for the highest rookie batting average ever. He dominated the sport throughout his career. Jackson deserves to be in the Hall of Fame. He earned the honor with his unequaled performance on the field.

B. Study the FATP chart below. Then read the essay at right and answer the questions.

FATP Chart

Form: *inspirational essay*

Audience: *classmates*

Topic: *Jim Abbott*

Purpose: *to inspire*

1. Is the writer's tone appropriate for the audience and purpose? Explain your answer.

____

____

____

____

____

____

____

____

2. Does the word choice seem appropriate for an inspirational essay? Explain your answer.

____

____

____

____

____

____

____

3. If you answered yes to Item 2, circle examples of appropriate voice in the text. If you answered no, use revising marks to show how you would change it.

Jim Abbott

Jim Abbott was born in 1967 with no right hand. His right arm ended at the wrist. It would have been easy for him to use his disability as an excuse to not get involved with sports. Instead, Abbott became an award-winning professional athlete.

In 1988, Abbott pitched for the U.S. Olympic baseball team, winning a gold medal. He went on to play professional baseball for 11 years.

As a one-handed pitcher, Abbott would balance his glove on his right arm while he pitched with his left hand. After throwing the ball, he would slide his left hand into the glove. If he fielded a ball, he could hold his glove between his right forearm and torso, take his left hand out, grab the ball, and throw it. He could do all of this as fast as any two-handed player.

On September 4, 1993, Abbott pitched a no-hitter against the Cleveland Indians.

Abbott has won numerous awards during his collegiate and professional sports careers. He has also inspired countless other disabled athletes.

Name ______________________ Date ______________

Use Figurative Language

A. An idiom is a familiar expression that's not literally true. Explain the meaning of each underlined idiom.

1. "You really dropped the ball on this one," I told Dmitri when I found out he had forgotten his part of the project. ______________________

2. Some people are born with a silver spoon in their mouths; others are born with two strikes against them. ______________________

3. "The teacher loved your presentation! You really hit a home run this time." ______________________

4. I was worried about the test, but Mr. Jones promised he wouldn't throw us any curveballs. ______________________

B. A simile compares two things using the words *like* or *as*. Write what you think each simile means.

1. Outfielder Ichiro Suzuki's arm is like a rocket. ______________________

2. The record holder for the most stolen bases, Rickey Henderson could run like a cheetah. ______________________

3. Baseball can be as exciting as winning the lottery and as heartbreaking as watching your dog die. ______________________

4. She leapt through the air and caught the ball like a frog snagging a fly with its tongue. ______________________

C. A metaphor compares two things by saying one thing *is* the other thing. Write what you think each metaphor means.

1. His glove was a magnet.

____

____

2. Baseball to her was breath and food and water.

____

____

3. The team was a well-conducted orchestra.

____

____

4. The roar of the fans was thunder in his ears.

____

____

D. Write an example of a simile, metaphor, and idiom. Be sure to explain what they mean!

Idiom: ____

____

Explanation: ____

____

Simile: ____

____

Explanation: ____

____

Metaphor: ____

____

Explanation: ____

____

Name ____________________ Date ____________

Plan a Biography

Use pages 189–190 to plan your biography.

1. Choose your topic, audience, and purpose. Fill out the FATP chart below.

FATP Chart

Form: biography

Audience: ____________________

Topic: ____________________

____

____

Purpose: ____________________

____

____

2. Decide what's most important to say about the subject's life. Do research to check your facts and fill in missing details. Use the space below for notes from your research.

3. Use the sequence chain to organize your thoughts.

Beginning

Events

Ending

Sequence Chain

Name ______________________ Date ______________

Draft a Biography

Use your plan from pages 189–190 to write the first draft of your biography.

Drafting Checklist

- ☐ Catch the reader's interest in your introduction.
- ☐ Include background information about your subject.
- ☐ Tell about important events in your subject's life, in chronological order.
- ☐ Include sequence words and dates to show the order of events.
- ☐ End by explaining why the subject is important.

Name ______________________ Date ____________

Revise a Biography

1. Use the checklist to evaluate this draft of a biography. What changes are needed?

____

____

____

____

____

Revising Checklist

- ❑ Are there any unnecessary details or repeated ideas?
- ❑ Can you combine any sentences?
- ❑ Can you use more colorful or specific language?
- ❑ Can you consolidate any ideas?
- ❑ Can you add any details to clarify ideas?

2. Revise the draft. Use revising marks to show your changes.

Revising

MARK	WHAT IT MEANS
^	Insert something.
↶⬭	Move to here.
⌃‾	Replace with this.
⌒	Take out.
¶	Make a new paragraph.

The Iron Horse of Baseball

Lou Gehrig, one of baseball's best players, was born in 1903. His parents encouraged him to get an education. Gehrig was naturally athletic, though. Gehrig joined the major leagues in 1923. In 1939, he retired with one of baseball's best records. His achievements still haven't been beaten by anyone else.

Gehrig is well known for working hard, being persistent, and for his batting record. His record of 2,130 consecutive played games wasn't broken for years. He still holds the record for most grand slams ever hit.

3. Now use the checklist to help you revise the draft of your biography on pages 191–192.

Edit and Proofread

Grammar Workout: Check Consistency in Verb Tenses

Complete each sentence with the correct tense of the verb in parentheses.

1. Dottie didn't know many people at first, but she quickly ______________ (learn) everyone's name.

2. Dottie ______________ (be) so nice, she made friends with all the players.

3. When they ______________ (see) her fielding skills, everyone was impressed.

4. When you see a great player scoop up a ground ball, you ______________ (feel) like you're watching an artist at work.

5. That's how I ______________ (feel) when I saw old movies of Dottie on the field.

6. Dottie's reputation ______________ (continue) to grow as more fans get to know her story.

Spelling Workout: Check Words with Silent Consonants

Circle the correct spelling of the word in each sentence.

1. Something **new/knew** happened in the world of baseball during World War II.

2. The men were away at war, and baseball owners **restled/wrestled** with the idea of having women play pro ball.

3. The time seemed **right/wright** to allow women to get their turn.

4. "We **now/know** the game as well as the men," women players argued.

5. At first, the public thought there was something **rong/wrong** with women playing professional baseball.

6. In the end, both the owners and the fans gave enthusiastic **thums/thumbs** up to the idea.

Name ______________________________ Date ______________

Mechanics Workout: Check Semicolons

Use proofreading marks to insert a semicolon where necessary.

1. Dottie enjoyed spring training in Havana. she loved to travel!

2. Dottie had a strict work ethic she couldn't accept people "not giving their best."

3. Dottie never stopped loving baseball. When she was 65, she responded to a questionnaire with the comment, "Loved the game and still do."

4. Dottie was the youngest player to play in the AAGPBL, at only 15 years old, she was so young she had to get her mother's permission to be able to play.

5. Dottie was the most photographed player in the league and signed the most autographs, but she was known as the most modest player as well.

Check Grammar, Spelling, and Mechanics

Proofread the passage. Check the spelling and the consistency of verb tenses. Correct the mistakes. Also, combine some sentences using semicolons.

Editing and Proofreading Marks

∧	Insert something.
∧,	Add a comma.
∧;	Add a semicolon.
⊙	Add a period.
(:)	Add a colon.
∨" ∨"	Add quotation marks.
∨'	Add an apostrophe.
≡	Capitalize.
/	Make lowercase.
℘	Delete.
¶	Make new paragraph.
◯	Spell out.
∧‾	Replace with this.
∿	Change order.
#	Insert space.
⁀‿	Close up.

Dottie Schroeder was one of the great athletes of the 20th century. Because she was incredibly talented, as well as attractive and friendly, she becomes an instant fan favorite. But if she new she was a star, she didn't show it. She was always modest and friendly to everyone.

After she retired from baseball, Dottie lives with her brother in Champaign, Illinois. She couldn't rap her head around a wrestful retirement, though. She worked nonstop for the next 36 years.

Edit and Proofread Your Biography

Now edit and proofread your work.

Remember to Check

- ☐ consistency of verb tenses
- ☐ spelling of words with silent consonants
- ☐ semicolons
- ☐ ______________________
- ☐ ______________________

1. Use a checklist as you edit and proofread. Add things you are working on to the checklist.

2. Look to see which errors are marked most often. Jot down your top three trouble spots.

____

____

____

3. Ask your teacher about ways to fix these mistakes, or check out the Grammar Handbook for information.

Focus on Spelling

Improve your spelling by following these steps.

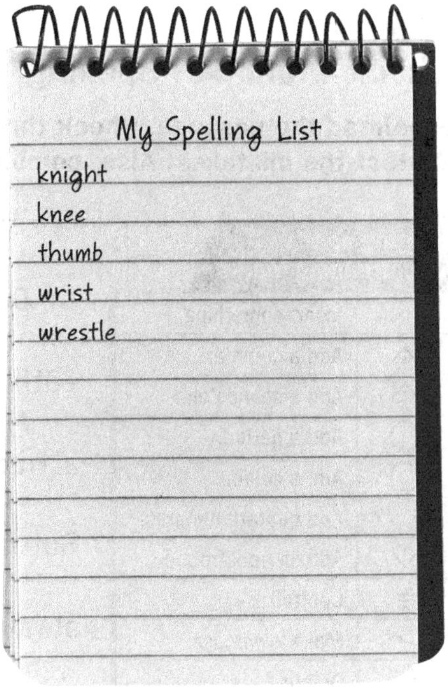

1. Create a personal spelling list. Record words that you misspelled. Look up correct spelling in the dictionary and add these words to **My Spelling List**.

2. Pick twelve words. Write each word four times. First write it in all lowercase letters. Next write it in all capital letters. After that, write the vowels in lowercase and the consonants in capital letters. Last, write the word using fancy letters that you create on your own. For example, your letters can be curly or tall and skinny.

3. Work with a partner to play **I'm Thinking of a Spelling Word**. Take turns giving each other clues. Some clues might be *I'm thinking of a word that rhymes with . . .*, *I'm thinking of a word that begins with . . .*, or *I'm thinking of a word that means . . .* With each clue, the answer should include the word and its spelling.

4. Play a scrambled-letter game with a partner. Take each other's spelling words and write them in scrambled form. See who can unscramble all the words first.

5. Use an audio recorder and record your words and their spelling. Then listen to your recording, checking to see that you spelled each word correctly.

Name ______________________ Date ______________

Publish, Share, and Reflect

Publish and Share Your Biography

Check the final formats you used to publish your biography. Then answer the following questions.

Publishing

What was the final format of your project?

- ☐ Wrote it neatly by hand
- ☐ Typed it on a computer

How did you share your project?

- ☐ Shared it with a large group
- ☐ Shared it with a small group

1. Whether you published it by hand or on the computer, what did you do to dress up your final project?

____

____

____

____

____

2. How did you share your work? What did you learn through sharing your work?

____

____

____

____

____

____

____

____

____

____

____

____

____

____

Reflect on Your Biography

Read your biography. Then answer questions 1–6.

1. What do you like best about your work? ______________________

____

____

2. What did you do well? ______________________

____

____

3. What could you improve about your work? ______________________

____

____

____

4. Does your biography show why your subject's life is important? ______________________

____

____

5. Did your own voice come through in your writing? ______________________

____

____

6. Will you add your biography to your Writing Portfolio? Explain your decision.

- ☐ Yes, I will add this to my Writing Portfolio.

  ____

  ____

- ☐ No, I will not add this to my Writing Portfolio.

  ____

  ____

Name ____________________ Date ____________

Analyze a Public Service Announcement

What makes an effective public service announcement? Read the models and answer the questions.

Deforestation in the United States

Our forests are being destroyed too fast for them to recover. Deforestation in the United States has resulted in the loss of 90% of its untouched forests since the 1600s. Landowners are offered money for their trees. Companies want to cut down the trees to make wood products. It takes more than 100 years for the area to recover. Not all areas can recover. Landowners sell the empty land to companies that want to build houses.

Interest in the environment has led people to try to repair the damage. People are planting trees, repopulating forests, and trying to replace lost habitats.

Save the Rainforest!

What would happen if we lost Earth's rainforests? Most rainforests are thousands of miles away from us. You might not know much about them. Even so, it's important for us to care about them. Why? The destruction of rainforests has a major impact on our planet's health.

Rainforests help the Earth stay in balance. For example, the tall, emerald green trees that grow in the rainforest use their giant leaves to prevent excess water from reaching the ground. Without the trees' help, too much water would reach the ground quickly, causing mudslides or flooding.

Feature Checklist

A good public service announcement

- ☐ captures the listener's interest with a clearly stated position
- ☐ tells how the position differs from alternate or opposing positions
- ☐ supports the position with logical reasons and relevant evidence
- ☐ uses transition words and phrases
- ☐ concludes with a call to action that supports the position.

1. Compare the two passages. Which passage captures your interest? How?

____

____

____

____

____

2. What position do the writers of both passages take?

____

____

____

____

3. Which passage provides better support for its position? Explain.

____

____

____

____

____

____

Write Effective Sentences

Vary Your Sentences

Rewrite the paragraph using the Recipe for Sentence Variety.

In big cities, pollution is a problem. People should make changes to reduce pollution. To help decrease pollution, some people ride bikes to school or work. If people have to drive, they can carpool to save gas. Buses and other public transportation also help. Many cities also have hybrid or electric buses. Telecommuting may be the best solution.

Recipe for Sentence Variety:

- Keep some sentences short and sweet.
- Craft some longer, "meaty" sentences, too.
- Consider adding a fragment or two—but don't overuse them.

Name ______________________________ Date ______________

Write Effective Sentences, continued

Streamline Your Sentences

Rewrite the paragraph to make the sentences more streamlined.

Ways to Streamline Sentences

- cut down wordiness
- combine sentences with appositives.

The state legislature will hear testimony on pesticide use this week, and members of the public are invited to speak. The debate over pesticides is a heated one. A large number of people say that pesticides harm the environment and people. Pat Augustine thinks that pesticides should be banned. She is a 34-year-old mother who has three children. Due to the fact that she buys a lot of produce for her children, she is concerned that the pesticides will have harmful effects on their health. Michael Grant disagrees. He is a farmer from Middleton, Illinois. He needs pesticides to protect his crops from insects. In this day and age, the majority of farms would not be able to function without pesticides.

Keep Your Sentences Parallel

Rewrite the paragraph to make the sentences parallel.

Oil spills are dangerous. They can harm animals, people, and where important marine life exists. There are ways to prevent oil spills, such as tightening requirements and replace oil tankers with double-hulled ships. A double hull puts an extra barrier between the oil and outside of the ship. This lowers the risk of an oil spill. If a double-hulled ship collides with sharp rocks, then damaging would most likely be occurring only on the outside hull. It would not harm the inside hull. The oil would be protected.

To Keep Sentences Parallel

- use the same grammatical form for similar items within a sentence.

Name ______________________ Date ______________

Plan a Public Service Announcement

Use pages 203–204 to plan your public service announcement.

1. Write down some issues you feel strongly about, either for or against.

Ideas/Issues

2. Pick your three best ideas or issues. List the good and bad points of each. Then circle the issue that you want to write about.

Ideas/Issues	Good and Bad Points

3. Write your opener. Include an attention-getting first sentence and a clear statement of your position.

4. Organize your support. List your evidence in order of strength. Then write an objection to it and a counterclaim or rebuttal.

Strong Reason →	Objection →	Counterclaim/ Rebuttal
Stronger Reason →	Objection →	Counterclaim/ Rebuttal
Strongest Reason →	Objection →	Counterclaim/ Rebuttal

Name ______________________ Date ______________

Draft a Public Service Announcement

Use your plan from pages 203–204 to write the first draft of your public service announcement.

Drafting Checklist

- [ ] Capture the listeners' interest.
- [ ] Clearly state your position.
- [ ] Distinguish your position from opposing views.
- [ ] Support your position with logical reasons and relevant evidence.
- [ ] Use transition words to connect your ideas.
- [ ] Conclude with a call to action that supports your position.

Name ______________________ Date ______________

Revise a Public Service Announcement

1. Use the checklist to evaluate this draft of a public service announcement. What changes are needed?

____

____

____

____

____

____

____

____

Revising Checklist

- ☐ Do you capture the listeners' interest?
- ☐ Do you clearly state your position?
- ☐ Do you tell how your position differs from opposing views?
- ☐ Do you support your position with logical reasons and relevant evidence?
- ☐ Do you use transition words and phrases?
- ☐ Do you conclude with a statement that supports your position?

2. Revise the draft. Use revising marks to show your changes.

Revising

MARK	WHAT IT MEANS
^	Insert something.
(loop with arrow)	Move to here.
(caret with line)	Replace with this.
(line with loop)	Take out.
¶	Make a new paragraph.

The Hidden Risk

Radon is a problem. You should learn about it and have your home tested for it. This invisible, odorless, tasteless gas might be putting you and your family at higher risk for cancer. There are many types of cancer. Many homes have too much radon. Many people get sick from radon. The good news is that testing for and fixing radon problems is usually easy and not too expensive. Test your home today.

3. Now use the checklist to help you revise the draft of your public service announcement on pages 205–206. Use a clean sheet of paper.

Edit and Proofread

Grammar Workout: Check Present Perfect Tense

Complete each sentence with the present perfect tense of the verb in parentheses.

1. Plastic ____________________ (contribute) significantly to the amount of trash in landfills.

2. For years, environmentalists ____________________ (try) to get people to cut down on the use of plastic.

3. Many towns ____________________ (begin) to recycle plastic bottles.

4. I ____________________ (bring) my own water bottle to school instead of buying bottled water.

5. Our local grocery store ____________________ (replace) plastic bags with reusable canvas sacks.

Spelling Workout: Use Spelling Rules

Find the spelling error in each sentence. Write the misspelled word correctly.

1. For many years, my friends and I have playied at community parks.

2. I think the parks in many of those communitys need recycling bins.

3. So, I am tring to get others to agree with me.

4. Maybe we can spend a few daes collecting donations at the entrances to the park.

5. I, for one, would be a lot happyier knowing that I helped the environment.

Name ______________________________ Date ______________

Mechanics Workout: Commas Between Adjectives

Read each sentence. Add any necessary commas.

1. I talked to my favorite next-door neighbor about my plan.

2. He suggested that we write a serious persuasive letter to the city.

3. We felt that our thoughtful dedicated mayor would approve our plan.

4. Maybe the city would help us set up local donation centers.

5. I hope that the mayor says "yes" to our simple unique plan.

Check Grammar, Spelling, and Mechanics

Proofread the passage. Check the spelling, use of verbs in the present perfect tense, and commas between adjectives. Correct the mistakes.

Editing and Proofreading Marks

∧	Insert something.
∧ with comma	Add a comma.
∧ with semicolon	Add a semicolon.
⊙	Add a period.
(:)	Add a colon.
∨ with quotation marks	Add quotation marks.
∨ with apostrophe	Add an apostrophe.
≡	Capitalize.
/	Make lowercase.
℘	Delete.
¶	Make new paragraph.
◯	Spell out.
∧‾	Replace with this.
∿	Change order.
#	Insert space.
⁀	Close up.

My friends and I have go to community parks for years. Since we were very young boyes, we have played baseball there. We have chased each other through the green grass. Even my mom have jogged on its wide paved path. And my sister has studyed under the shade of the trees. But, unfortunately, many of these peaceful lovely parks has become unsafe and ugly because of all the litter and trash. The city has promises to do something about the problem. We certainly hope they are triing! Everyone needs a clean, beautiful place to relax.

Edit and Proofread Your Public Service Announcement

Now edit and proofread your work.

Remember to Check

- ☐ present perfect tense
- ☐ spelling of words ending in *-y*
- ☐ commas between adjectives
- ☐ ______________________
- ☐ ______________________

1. Use a checklist as you edit and proofread. Add things you are working on to the checklist.

2. Look to see which errors are marked most often. Jot down your top three trouble spots.

   ____

   ____

   ____

3. Ask your teacher about ways to fix these mistakes, or check out the Grammar Handbook for information.

Focus on Spelling

Improve your spelling by following these steps.

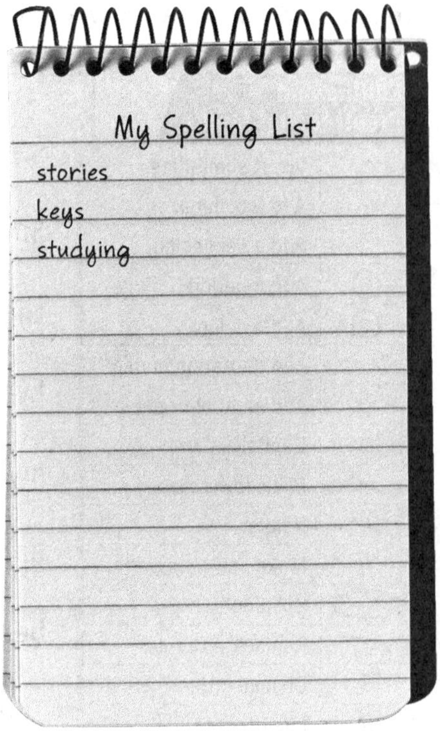

1. Create a personal spelling list. Record words that you misspelled. Look up correct spelling in the dictionary and add these words to **My Spelling List**.

2. Pick twelve words. Make each word look interesting and special by tracing it five times. Write the word in one color. Then trace it four more times in four different colors. Say each letter to yourself as you trace it.

3. Work with a partner to play **Spelling Catch**. Pitch words to each other by saying "Here's the windup. Here's the pitch. The word is . . ." Take turns pitching. The first "batter" to spell all ten words correctly wins.

4. Write each spelling word three times. The first time, just write the word. The second time, write it and then circle all the consonants. The third time, write it and circle all the vowels.

5. Play **Memory** to help you remember the words. Write each spelling word on two different index cards. Mix up the cards and place them face down. Turn the cards over two at a time. Your goal is to find the matching cards. Say and spell the words on the cards you turn over. If you make a match, remove those cards from the game. You've won when you've removed all the cards.

Name ______________________ Date ______________

Analyze a Persuasive Essay

What makes this persuasive essay a good model? Read the essay and answer the questions.

Recycling

by Kylie Green

Many Americans have started recycling to help conserve resources and protect the environment. Unfortunately, each year people create more and more trash. Trash that isn't recycled is taken to landfills and buried. Scientists still don't know all of the effects of burying garbage underground, or what it does to plants and animals. Only time will tell. We do know that recycling is a way to limit the amount of trash being sent to landfills.

Recycling has many environmental and economic benefits. It saves natural resources and energy, reduces air and water pollution, and creates jobs. When you recycle you are remaking an old item to use again. This helps the environment by conserving natural resources. For example, one ton of recycled paper can save up to 17 trees! Recycling also saves energy. The process of creating a new product from recycled materials can use up to 95% less energy than creating the same product from natural resources. That's a lot of saved energy! Recycling materials is a complicated process. People are needed to collect, sort, and create products. This creates five times more jobs than regular garbage disposal. In fact, more than a million jobs in America are connected to recycling.

Feature Checklist

A good persuasive essay

- ❑ states the writer's position on the issue
- ❑ appeals to logic using evidence
- ❑ appeals to emotions using persuasive language
- ❑ addresses the opposing argument
- ❑ ends with a call to action.

1. **What is the writer's position on the issue?**

____

____

____

____

____

2. **What reasons does the writer give to support her position?**

____

____

____

____

____

3. **What evidence does the writer use to make a logical appeal?**

____

____

____

____

____

____

____

People who oppose recycling point out that recycling isn't cheap. It can cost more to recycle than create new products from natural resources. The cost to keep open recycling centers can be high too. It's true that recycling is neither free nor cheap, but is it acceptable to pollute the Earth because it saves you money? What is the cost to the environment not to recycle? The role of recycling is not necessarily to save money. It's to save the Earth. A glass bottle in a landfill is just trash that will sit there. However, that same glass bottle can be recycled over and over again so it never becomes trash to begin with.

Whether you're willing to drive to a drop-off location or take out the trash, there is a way for you to recycle. The most popular way to recycle is with a pick-up service. Cities set up pick-up schedules. Then people put out their recycling for collectors. It's just like taking out the garbage. All people have to do is separate their recycling into categories, such as paper, glass, and aluminum.

If we work together, we can hold on to our natural resources and not pollute the environment. Encouraging family and friends to recycle more is just the beginning. You can start a recycling program at school or your community center. You can spread the word that recycling helps the environment, and that is priceless.

4. How does the writer address the opposing argument?

____

____

____

____

____

____

____

5. How does the writer make an emotional appeal?

____

____

____

____

____

____

____

6. How does the essay end?

____

____

____

____

____

____

____

____

____

Name ______________________________ Date ______________

Appeal to Logic

Read the paragraph. Then rewrite it to include appeals to logic. Use information from the Evidence Bank to support your argument.

Say No to Plastic Bags

Americans use lots of plastic shopping bags. But plastic bags are terrible for the environment. They create problems for people and animals. That's why we should work to reduce the number of plastic bags we use every day. Shoppers should take reusable cloth bags to the store. Cloth totes are the most environmentally friendly bags available. Stores can also discourage plastic-bag use by charging extra for plastic bags. If enough people follow these suggestions, we can make our planet a better, cleaner place to live.

Evidence Bank

- Americans throw away 100 billion plastic bags each year.
- About 100,000 ocean animals are killed by plastic bags each year.
- In the state of California, officials spend millions of dollars each year disposing of plastic bags and picking up plastic litter.
- In Ireland, a tax on plastic bags reduced plastic-bag use by over 90%.
- The environmental organization Green Group says that plastic bags are incredibly difficult to recycle, and most people don't try to recycle them anyway.
- Recycling Committee president Alicia Brown said, "Cloth bags are better than paper and plastic bags because they can be reused for years."

Appeal to Emotion

Read the paragraph. Then rewrite it to include appeals to emotion. Use persuasive language and (if possible) personal examples (make one up if you need to!) to support your argument.

Replacing Lightbulbs

Changing lightbulbs is one thing people can do to help the environment. Compact fluorescent bulbs (CFLs) are good alternatives to regular bulbs. These special bulbs can be easily found in stores. They last longer than regular bulbs and fit in most light fixtures. They are more expensive than regular bulbs, but they also use less electricity and last much longer. Over time, a compact fluorescent bulb pays for itself. Using more efficient bulbs means using less fossil fuel. That helps the planet.

Name ______________________ Date ______________

Support Your Arguments

This persuasive essay could be more effective. Read the essay. Then revise it by adding

- **supporting facts (You may need to do a little research.)**
- **details to clarify and elaborate**
- **persuasive language to convince the reader.**

Shorter Showers, Better Earth

Most people don't realize the effect their actions have on the environment. Everything we do has some type of effect on the Earth. Everyday activities affect the environment. These activities can have a harmful effect on the Earth. The good news is that by making a few small changes in our lifestyles, we can reduce that harm.

Most people will admit they're guilty of taking long showers. A long shower can waste 25–35 gallons of water. That means a four-person household uses a lot of water just on showers!

There are many things you can do to reduce the amount of water you use while showering. It might be hard to get used to at first.

Think about if everyone reduced the amount of water they use by 15 gallons. That would save a lot every time. Don't you think it's a good idea?

Use Charts, Tables, and Pictures

Read each argument on pages 216–217. Consider the graphics that could support each argument. Then circle the letter of the graphic that you think would best support the argument. Explain your choice.

1. We should concentrate on recycling paper, because paper makes up the biggest part of the trash at our school.

A. A picture of a trash can showing a lot of paper

B. A pie chart showing the proportion of paper compared to other kinds of trash

C. A graph showing how the total amount of trash has increased over the last five years

____

____

____

____

____

____

2. Because the amount of recycled material at our school has increased every year for the past five years, we should buy more recycling bins. That way, we can continue to recycle more and more material.

A. A graph showing how many pounds of material were recycled during each of the past five years

B. A table showing the cost of five different types of recycling bins

C. A pie chart showing the percentage of classrooms in the school that have recycling bins and the percentage of classrooms that do not have bins

____

____

____

____

____

____

Use Charts, Tables, and Pictures, continued

3. We should buy Separation Station recycling bins because, unlike regular recycling bins, they have individual sections for different types of materials, and each section is clearly labeled to make it easy for students to recycle correctly.

A. A table showing how many schools buy Separation Station recycling bins each year

B. A pie chart showing the percentage of recycled material that is glass, plastic, and paper

C. A picture of a recycling bin with clearly labeled sections and a picture of a regular, unlabeled recycling bin

____

____

____

____

____

____

4. We should start an advertising campaign about recycling at our school. At other schools, advertising campaigns have caused more people to recycle regularly, so a similar campaign at our school would probably get more people to recycle.

A. A picture of students hanging a sign that encourages people to recycle

B. A graph showing the number of students, faculty, and staff who report paying attention to school advertising campaigns

C. A table showing how many people at three schools with advertising campaigns recycled regularly before and after the campaigns

____

____

____

____

____

____

Plan a Persuasive Essay

Use pages 218–219 to plan your persuasive essay.

1. Jot down some issues that affect you or your community. Explain your position on each issue and what you want people to do about it. Then choose one issue to write about, and circle it.

Issues I Care About

2. Gather evidence to support your position. Write down the arguments you want to make in your essay. Then record evidence that supports each argument.

Argument	Evidence

Plan a Persuasive Essay, continued

3. Organize your main supporting points. Use the graphic organizer to identify your main position and your supporting reasons.

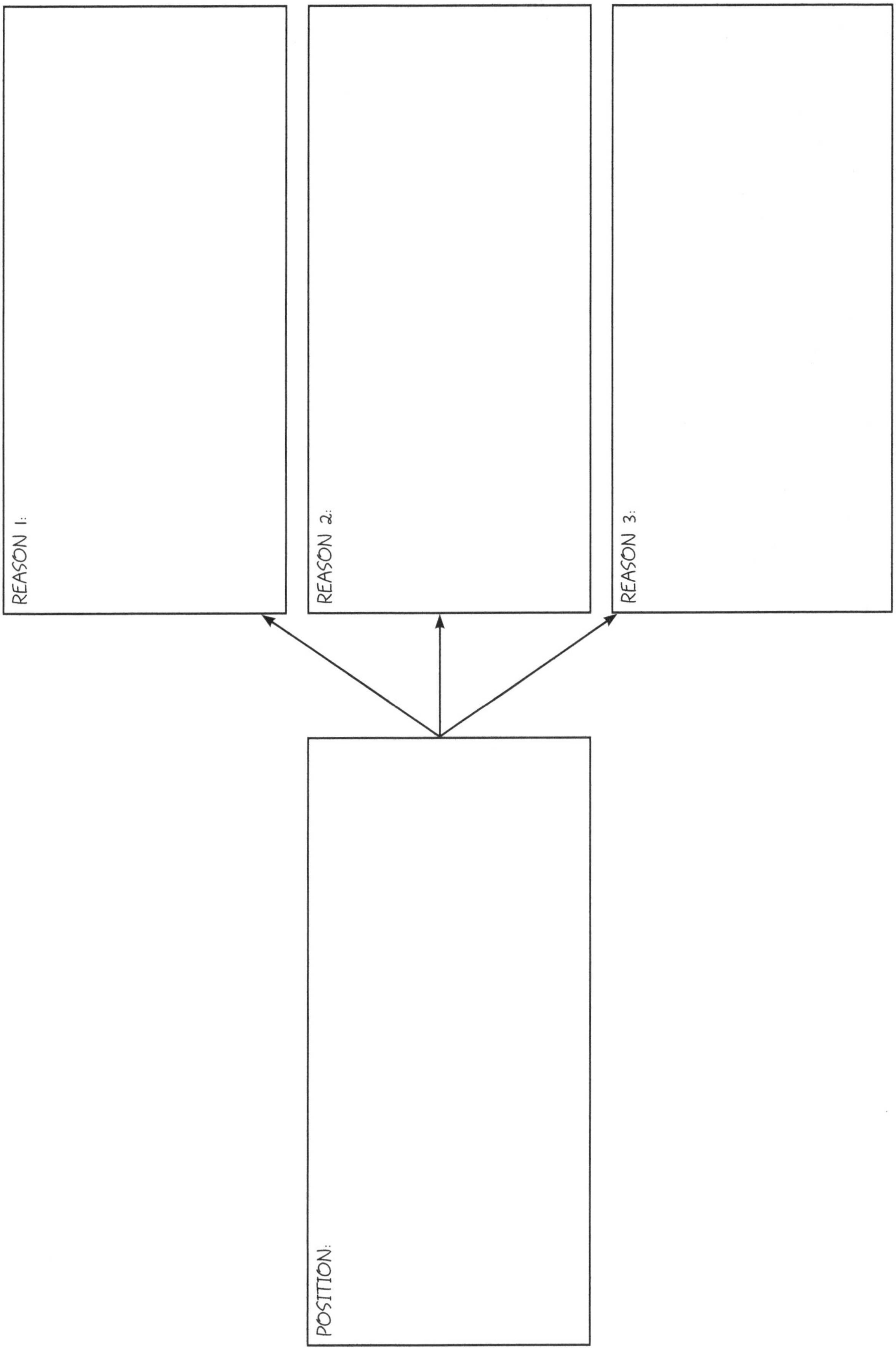

Draft a Persuasive Essay

Use your plan from pages 218–219 to write the first draft of your persuasive essay.

Drafting Checklist

- ☐ Clearly state your position in the introduction.
- ☐ Give background and reasons to support your position.
- ☐ Appeal to logic by using evidence.
- ☐ Appeal to emotions by using persuasive language.
- ☐ Strengthen your argument with charts, tables, and pictures.
- ☐ End with a strong call to action in the conclusion.

Name ____________________ Date __________

Draft a Persuasive Essay, continued

Revise a Persuasive Essay

1. Use the checklist to evaluate this draft of a persuasive essay. What changes are needed?

____

____

____

____

____

____

Revising Checklist

- ☐ Do you need to clarify your position with additional details or explanations?
- ☐ Can you streamline your essay by combining sentences?
- ☐ Can you make your ideas clearer with more colorful or precise language?
- ☐ Where can you delete repetitive or wordy phrases?

2. Revise the draft. Use revising marks to show your changes.

Revising

MARK	WHAT IT MEANS
∧	Insert something.
(move mark)	Move to here.
(replace mark)	Replace with this.
(delete mark)	Take out.
¶	Make a new paragraph.

Reuse Your Bags!

We should encourage people to carry reusable bags when they shop for groceries. Other countries, including China and Ireland, are taxing or outlawing the use of plastic and paper grocery bags. Both types have an impact on the environment. It's better to use other kinds.

Every year Americans throw away an incredible number of plastic grocery bags. They harm the environment. For instance, they pollute the oceans. Reusable grocery bags can dramatically reduce the amount of trash we produce. Consider making the change!

3. Now use the checklist to help you revise the draft of your persuasive essay on pages 220–221.

Name ______________________________ Date ______________

Edit and Proofread

Grammar Workout: Check Participial Phrases

Rewrite each sentence. Move the dangling participle or rephrase the sentence so the participial phrase describes the correct word.

1. Mrs. Thom found some cleansers looking around her home that weren't good for the environment.

____

2. Mrs. Thom cleaned with baking soda worried about harmful chemicals.

____

3. Baking soda removed some spots mixed with vinegar on her carpet.

____

4. Sprinkled on the carpet, the room started to smell fresh and clean.

____

5. Scrubbing sinks with baking soda, irritation on her hands was avoided.

____

Spelling Workout: Check Words with *q*, *ie*, and *ei*

Choose the correct spelling to complete each sentence.

1. What should you do when you're looking to ______________ (quench/qench) your thirst?

2. You may put some ______________ (quarters/qarters) in a vending machine for a bottled drink.

3. Vending-machine beverages may ______________ (releive/relieve) your thirst, but those plastic bottles take a toll on the environment.

4. The plastic bottles people throw out each year ______________ (weigh/wiegh) millions of pounds!

5. It's my ______________ (belief/beleif) that carrying reusable bottles would help.

Mechanics Workout: Participial Phrases and Appositives

Add the proper punctuation to each of these sentences containing participial phrases or appositives.

1. Hoping to foster environmental awareness our school started a recycling program.

2. Our principal Ms. Carlson talked about the program during a school assembly.

3. Recycling bins placed in every hallway remind students to recycle plastic bottles and metal cans.

4. Our teachers excited about the program have discussed recycling in class.

5. In science class, we watched a film about recycling "Reuse It or Lose It."

Check Grammar, Spelling, and Mechanics

Proofread the passage. Check the spelling, the use of participial phrases, and the commas with participial phrases and appositives. Correct the mistakes.

Editing and Proofreading Marks

^	Insert something.
^ (with comma)	Add a comma.
^ (with semicolon)	Add a semicolon.
⊙	Add a period.
(:)	Add a colon.
❛❛ ❜❜	Add quotation marks.
❜	Add an apostrophe.
≡	Capitalize.
/	Make lowercase.
℘	Delete.
¶	Make new paragraph.
◯	Spell out.
⌃—	Replace with this.
∽	Change order.
#	Insert space.
⁀‿	Close up.

Recently I learned qite a lot about caring for the environment. My science teacher Mr. Zahler created a whole unit about it. Spending a week about ways to recycle we were all able to pass the qiz on recycling. (I recieved an A.) We learned about environmental problems moving on to other topics. Studying global warming, we learned that the average temperature on Earth has risen by about one degree within the last century. You might not beleive that could have an impact, but it can. Glaciers have caused the average sea level to rise significantly melted by higher temperatures.

Name ______________________ Date ____________

Edit and Proofread, continued

Edit and Proofread Your Persuasive Essay

Now edit and proofread your work.

1. Use a checklist as you edit and proofread. Add things you are working on to the checklist.

2. Look to see which errors are marked most often. Jot down your top three trouble spots.

____

____

____

3. Ask your teacher about ways to fix these mistakes, or check out the Grammar Handbook for information.

Remember to Check

- ☐ participial phrases
- ☐ words with *q*, *ie*, and *ei*
- ☐ commas for participial phrases and appositives
- ☐ ______________
- ☐ ______________

Focus on Spelling

Improve your spelling by following these steps.

1. Create a personal spelling list. Record words that you misspelled. Look up correct spelling in the dictionary and add these words to **My Spelling List**.

2. Pick twelve words. Make each word look interesting and special by tracing it five times. Write the word in one color. Then trace it four more times in four different colors. Say each letter to yourself as you trace it.

3. Work with a partner to play **Spelling Catch**. Pitch words to each other by saying "Here's the windup. Here's the pitch. The word is . . ." Take turns pitching. The first "batter" to spell all ten words correctly wins.

4. Write each spelling word three times. The first time, just write the word. The second time, write it and then circle all the consonants. The third time, write it and circle all the vowels.

5. Play **Memory** to help you remember the words. Write each spelling word on two different index cards. Mix up the cards and place them face down. Turn the cards over two at a time. Your goal is to find the matching cards. Say and spell the words on the cards you turn over. If you make a match, remove those cards from the game. You've won when you've removed all the cards.

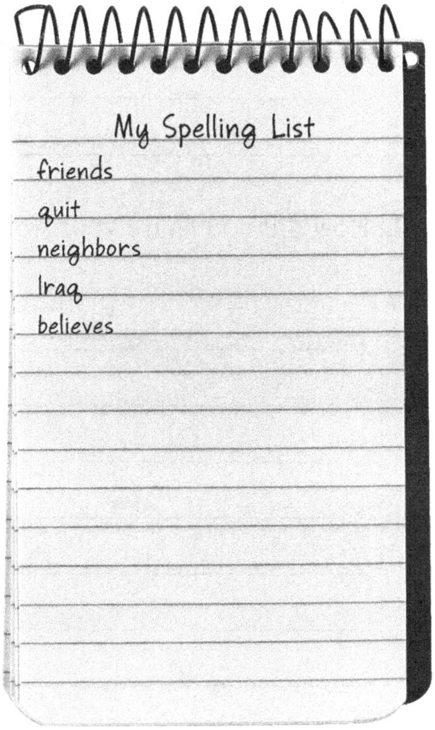

Publish, Share, and Reflect

Publish and Share Your Persuasive Essay

Check the final formats you used to publish your persuasive essay. Then answer the following questions.

Publishing

What was the final format of your project?	How did you share your project?
☐ Wrote it neatly by hand	☐ Shared it with a large group
☐ Typed it on a computer	☐ Shared it with a small group

1. Whether you published it by hand or on the computer, what did you do to dress up your final project?

2. How did you share your work? What did you learn through sharing your work?

Publish, Share, and Reflect, continued

Reflect on Your Persuasive Essay

Read your persuasive essay. Then answer questions 1–6.

1. What do you like best about your work? ______________________

2. What did you do well? ______________________

3. What could you improve about your work? ______________________

4. What did you learn about this issue from writing about it? ______________________

5. Has your position on this issue changed as a result of your writing about it? ______________________

6. Will you add your persuasive essay to your Writing Portfolio? Explain your decision.

☐ Yes, I will add this to my Writing Portfolio.

☐ No, I will not add this to my Writing Portfolio.